HUMAN BODY
THEATER

HUMAN BODY THEATER

Maris Wicks

First Second

New York

First Second

Copyright © 2015 by MARIS WICKS

Published by FIRST SECOND
First Second is an imprint of Roaring Brook Press,
a division of Holtzbrinck Publishing Holdings Limited Partnership
175 Fifth Avenue, New York, New York 10010
All rights reserved

Library of Congress Control Number: 2015937863

Paperback ISBN: 978-1-59643-929-0
Hardcover ISBN: 978-1-62672-277-4

First Second books may be purchased for business or promotional use.
For information on bulk purchases please contact Macmillan Corporate
and Premium Sales Department at (800) 221-7945 x5442 or
by email at specialmarkets@macmillan.com.

First edition 2015

Book design by Joyana McDiarmid
Printed in China by Macmillan Production (Asia) Ltd.,
Kowloon Bay, Hong Kong (supplier code 10)

Paperback: 10 9 8 7 6 5 4 3 2 1
Hardcover: 10 9 8 7 6 5 4 3 2 1

NOW SHOWING

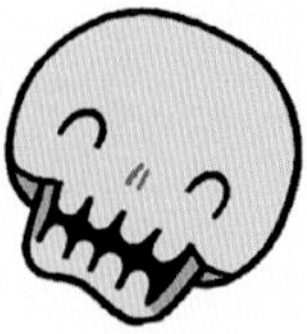

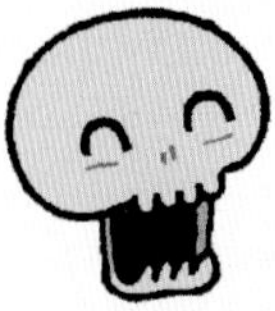

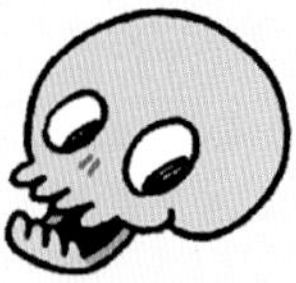

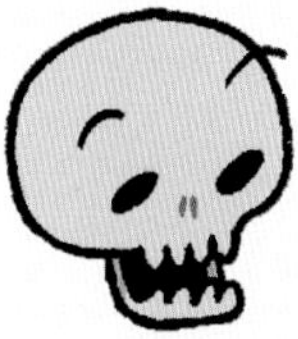

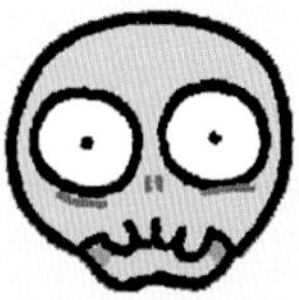

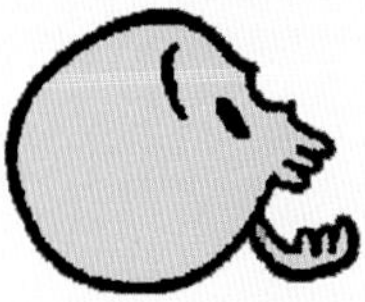

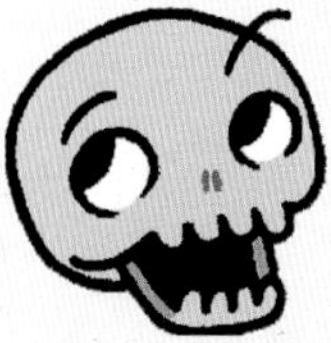

For Kira

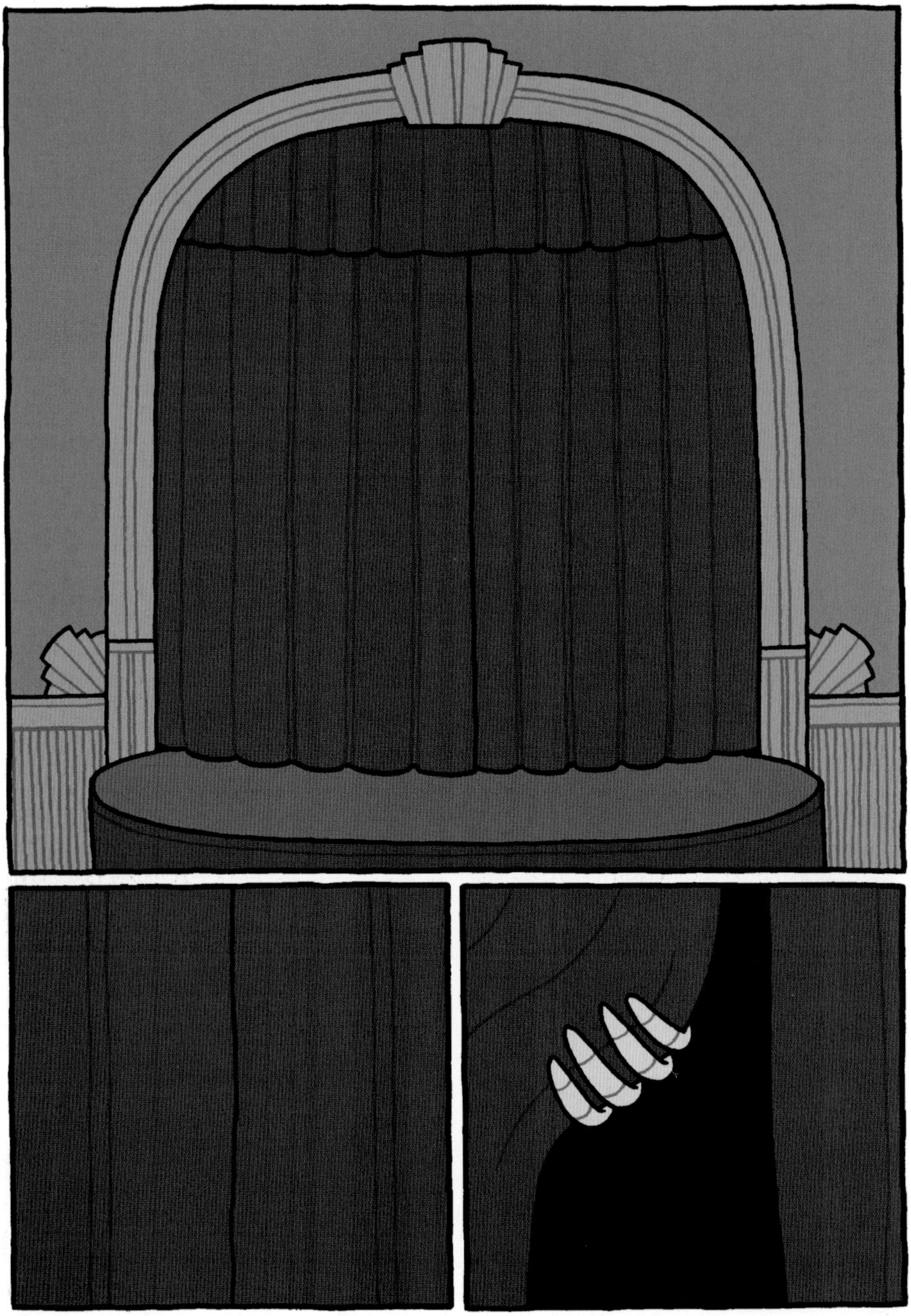

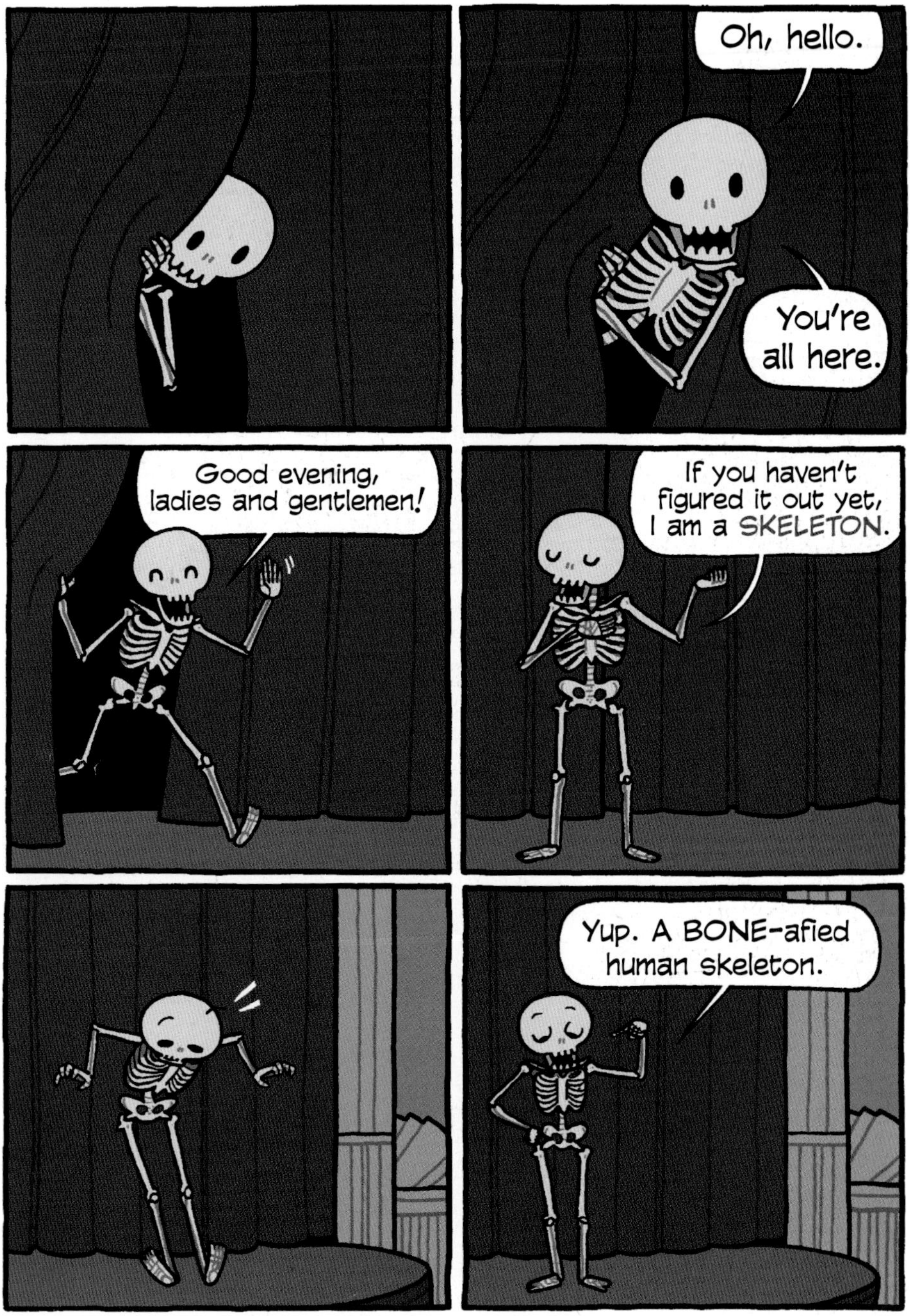
Oh, hello.
You're all here.
Good evening, ladies and gentlemen!
If you haven't figured it out yet, I am a SKELETON.
Yup. A BONE-afied human skeleton.

If you are concerned about my rather bare appearance, do not worry.

Over the course of this... er...performance, I will become fully formed.

There are a few additions that will help to make me look a bit more complete—

a HEART!

a BRAIN!

SOME LUNGS!

MUSCLES!

Right, right. But before we start all of that..

...I would like to introduce you to our hardworking stagehands:

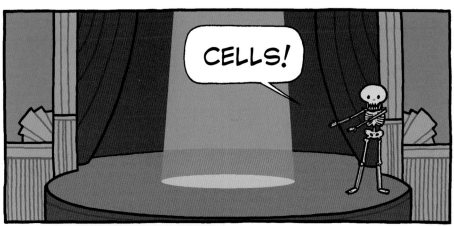

CELLS!

What's that? You can't see them?

Me neither.

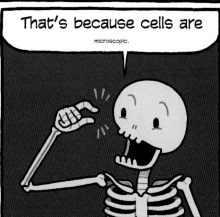

That's because cells are microscopic.

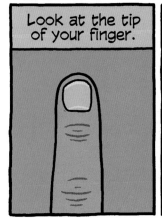

Look at the tip of your finger.

Now zoom in... 2,000 times!

It looks like this:

All living things (organisms) on this planet are made of these tiny structures called CELLS.

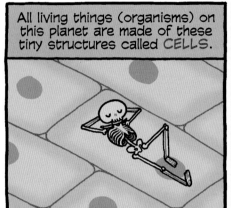

Our bodies have lots of different types of cells...

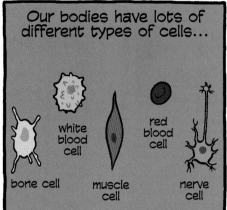

bone cell

white blood cell

muscle cell

red blood cell

nerve cell

LOOKING INSIDE: CELLS

...but almost all of these cells contain the same basic parts:

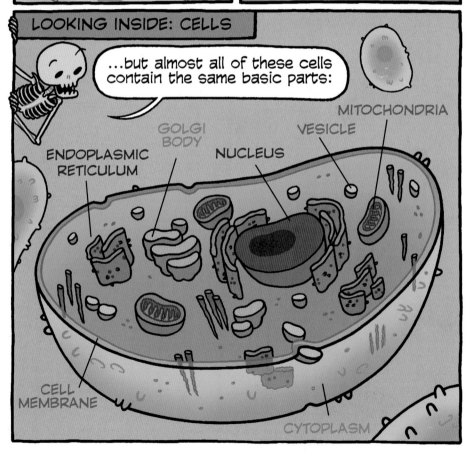

MITOCHONDRIA

GOLGI BODY

VESICLE

ENDOPLASMIC RETICULUM

NUCLEUS

CELL MEMBRANE

CYTOPLASM

The NUCLEUS contains the genetic instructions (DNA) for the cell.

The CYTOPLASM is the jellylike substance inside the cell.

MITOCHONDRIA provide energy for the cell.

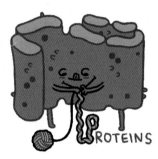

The ENDOPLASMIC RETICULUM makes proteins (like enzymes).

GOLGI BODIES package proteins into vesicles.

VESICLES leave the cell, carrying substances produced by the cell.

I'm going to let good ol' Golgi Body take it from here.

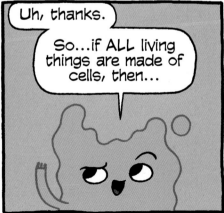

Uh, thanks.

So...if ALL living things are made of cells, then...

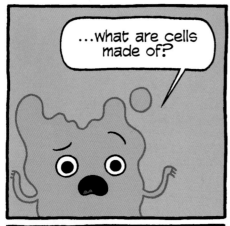

...what are cells made of?

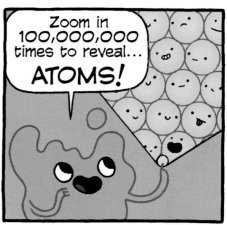

Zoom in 100,000,000 times to reveal... ATOMS!

ATOMS are the building blocks of all matter.

I matter!

Everything you see around you—your hand, this book—is made of atoms.

We're here!

Yeah, you just need a super-powerful electron miscroscope to see us!

There are many different types of atoms; they are called ELEMENTS.

Actually, every living thing is mostly made of 4 elements.

Hydrogen.

Oxygen!

Nitrogen ...

...and carbon.

Elementally speaking, this is what humans are made of:

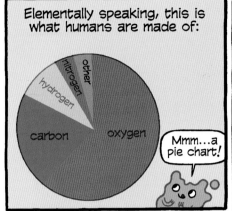

Mmm...a pie chart!

Now, this doesn't mean that your legs are made of oxygen.

All these elements mix and bond with one another to form the stuff of...us.

When 2 or more atoms are hanging out together, this is called a MOLECULE. And here is a molecule you all know:

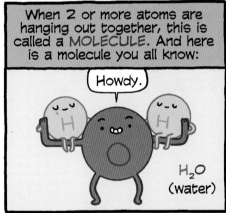

Howdy.

H_2O
(water)

And those molecules exist in one of 3 different STATES:

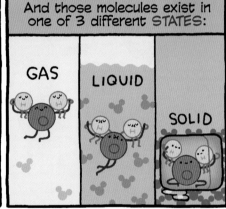

GAS

LIQUID

SOLID

Here are some other molecules you may be familiar with:

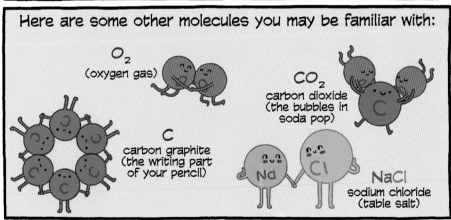

O_2
(oxygen gas)

CO_2
carbon dioxide
(the bubbles in soda pop)

C
carbon graphite
(the writing part
of your pencil)

$NaCl$
sodium chloride
(table salt)

It's not always that basic—
sometimes lots of atoms
make up one molecule:

$C_6H_{12}O_6$ (glucose)

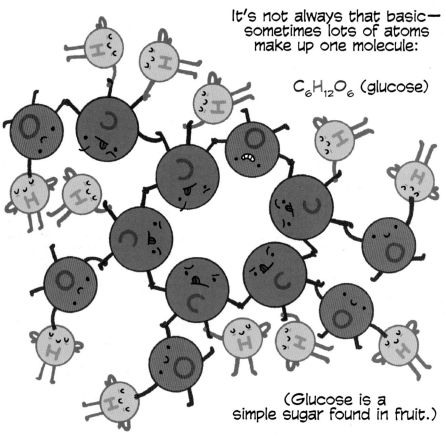

(Glucose is a
simple sugar found in fruit.)

Do you recognize the
individual elements in that
glucose molecule?

Our bodies are made
of hydrogen, oxygen,
nitrogen, and carbon...

...and we need to put
those very same elements
into our body to get
ENERGY.

I bet you'll never think
about eating the same
way again.

PROTEINS

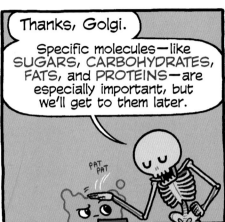

Thanks, Golgi.

Specific molecules—like SUGARS, CARBOHYDRATES, FATS, and PROTEINS—are especially important, but we'll get to them later.

PAT PAT

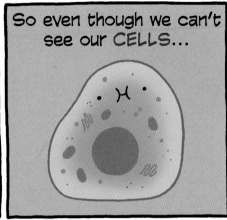

So even though we can't see our CELLS...

...MOLECULES...

...or ATOMS...

...they are there, running the show.

And, speaking of "show," I think we're just about ready.

Without further ado, I present to you—

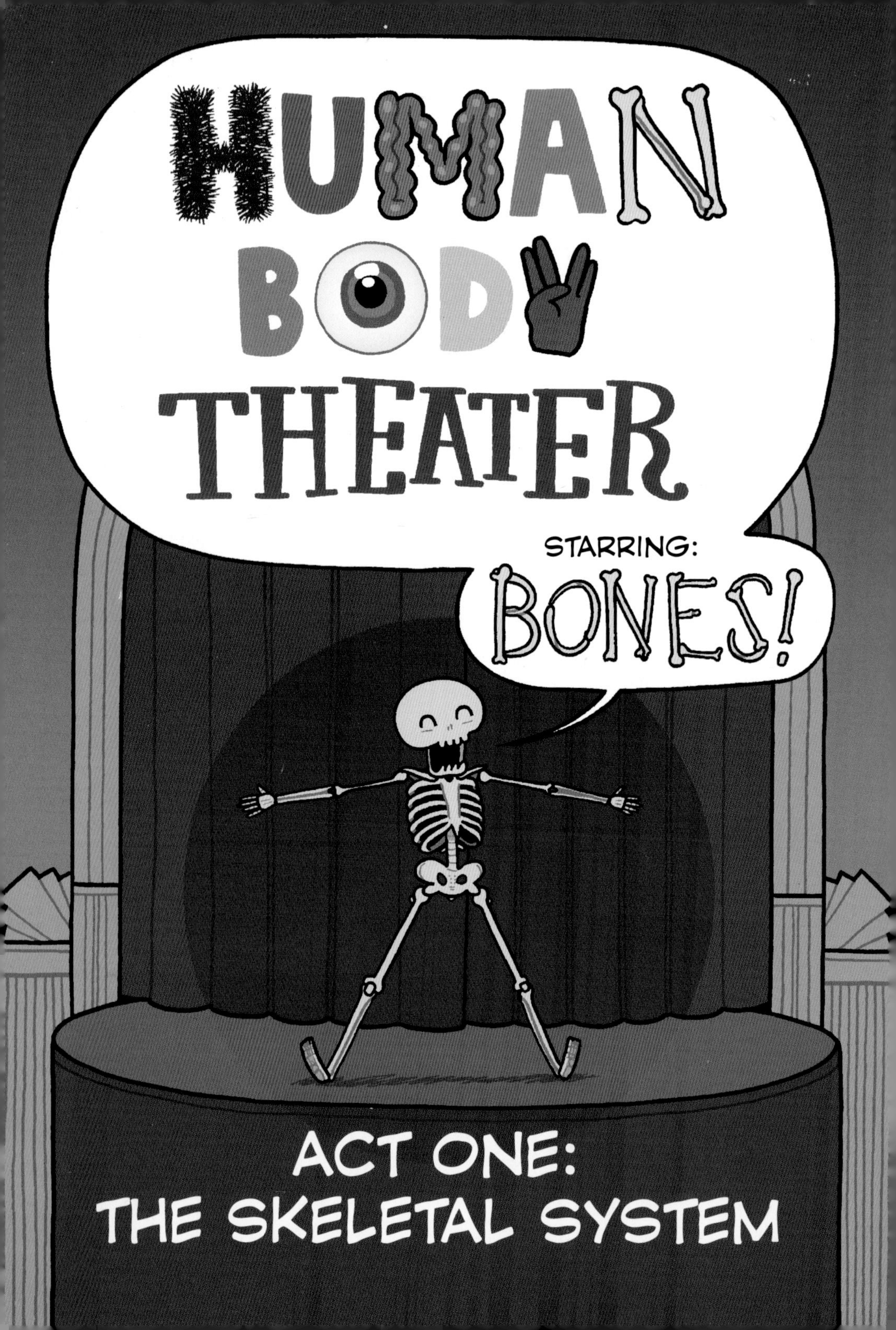
HUMAN BODY THEATER
STARRING:
BONES!
ACT ONE:
THE SKELETAL SYSTEM

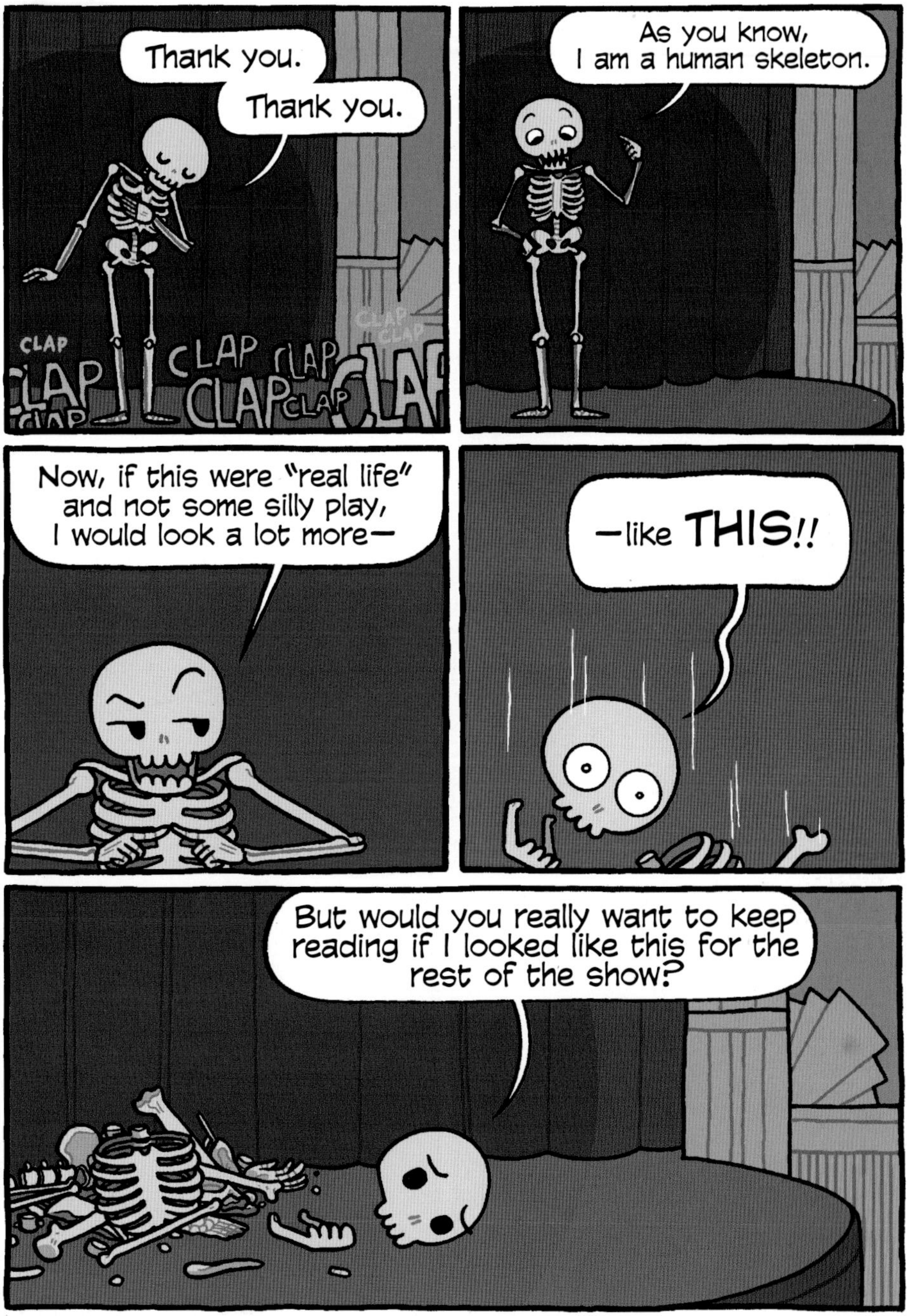
Thank you.
Thank you.
CLAP
CLAP
CLAP
CLAP
CLAP
CLAP
CLAP
CLAP
CLAP
As you know,
I am a human skeleton.
Now, if this were "real life" and not some silly play, I would look a lot more—
—like THIS!!
But would you really want to keep reading if I looked like this for the rest of the show?

I didn't think so.

Through the magic of pen and paper, I can be a standing, talking,

DANCING

BOO!!

skeleton.

Okay, fine. No dancing.

For now.

But I am going to tell you why bones are so—

BONE-Y?

—NO! Important.

BONES are the underlying structure for the whole human body.

When you look at the complex things that we humans build, you see how important an internal framework can be.

Without their underlying structures to support them, these objects would look a lot like me when I was a pile of bones— totally useless.

Our own bones work in a similar way—take a look:

There are 206 bones in the adult human body.

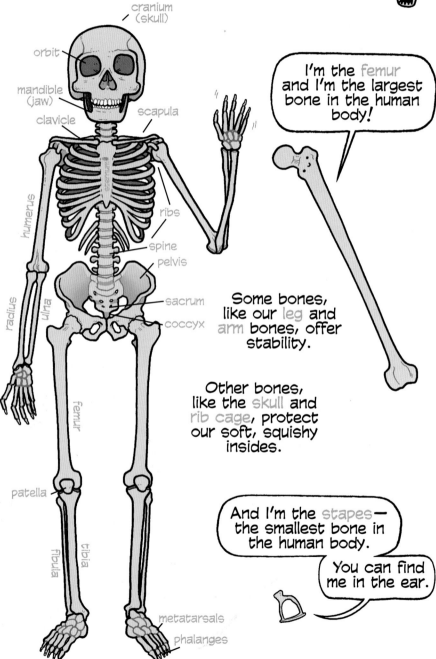

cranium
(skull)

orbit

mandible
(jaw)

clavicle

scapula

humerus

ribs

spine

pelvis

radius

ulna

sacrum

coccyx

femur

patella

fibula

tibia

metatarsals

phalanges

I'm the femur and I'm the largest bone in the human body!

Some bones, like our leg and arm bones, offer stability.

Other bones, like the skull and rib cage, protect our soft, squishy insides.

And I'm the stapes — the smallest bone in the human body.

You can find me in the ear.

LOOKING INSIDE: THE HAND AND THE FOOT

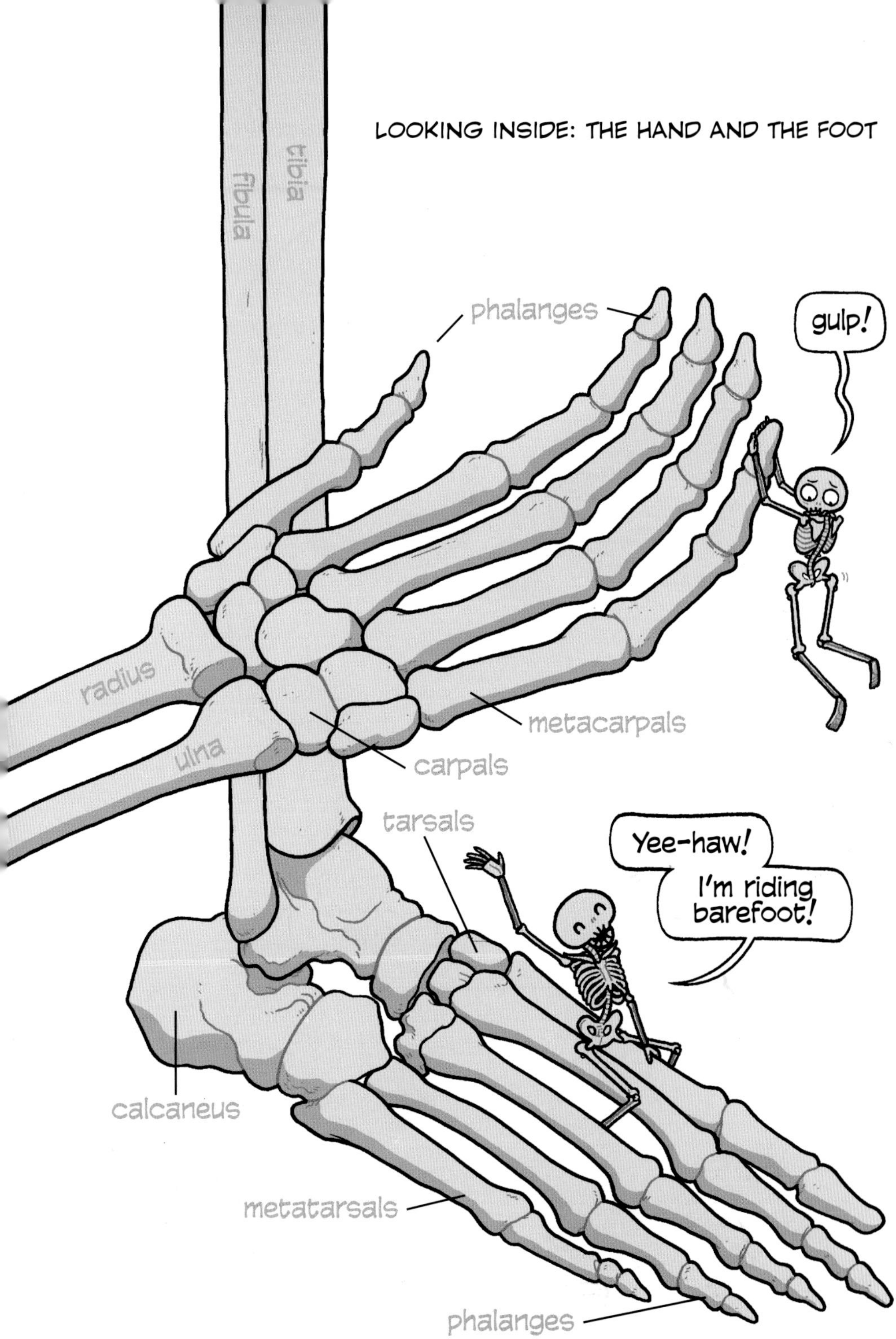
tibia
fibula
phalanges
gulp!
radius
ulna
carpals
metacarpals
tarsals
Yee-haw!
I'm riding barefoot!
calcaneus
metatarsals
phalanges

LOOKING INSIDE: THE SKULL

The skull houses the brain and keeps it safe...kind of like a built-in helmet!

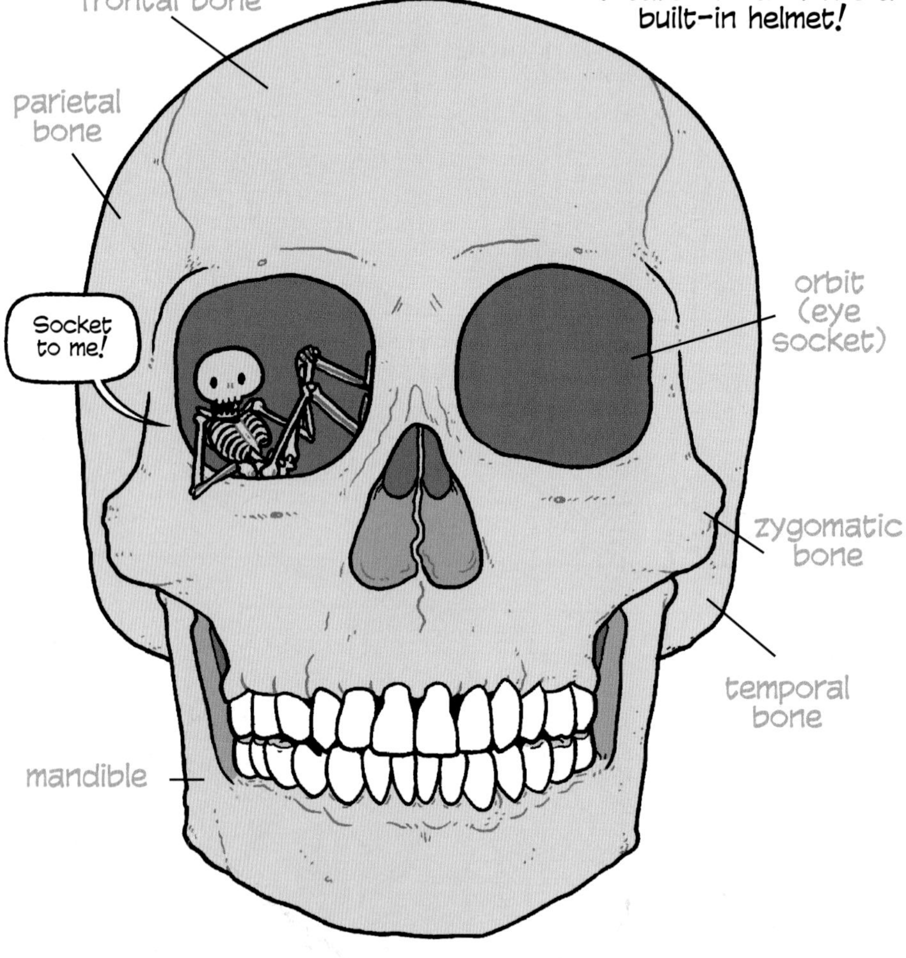
frontal bone
parietal bone
Socket to me!
orbit (eye socket)
zygomatic bone
temporal bone
mandible

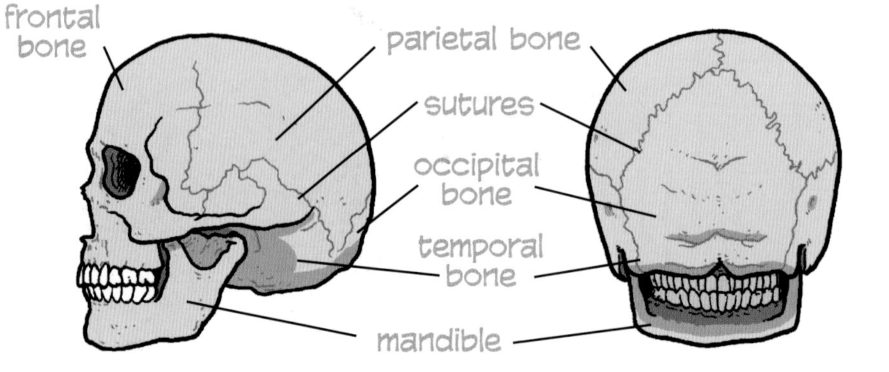
frontal bone
parietal bone
sutures
occipital bone
temporal bone
mandible

LOOKING INSIDE: THE SPINE

Each of the individual bones that make up the spine is called a vertebra, but a bunch of them together are called vertebrae.

This is quite a climb!

24 of the 33 vertebrae of the spine are connected with cushions of cartilage called spinal discs; this allows us to bend and twist.

The other 9 are fused together.

The spine also provides protection for a network of nerves called the spinal cord.

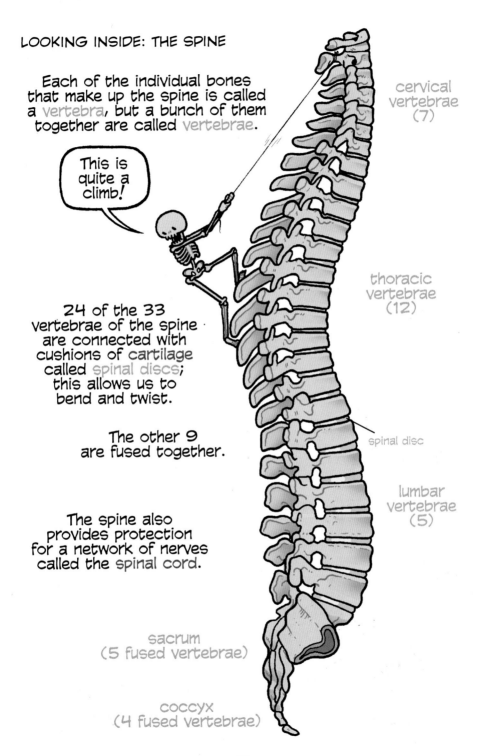

cervical vertebrae (7)

thoracic vertebrae (12)

spinal disc

lumbar vertebrae (5)

sacrum (5 fused vertebrae)

coccyx (4 fused vertebrae)

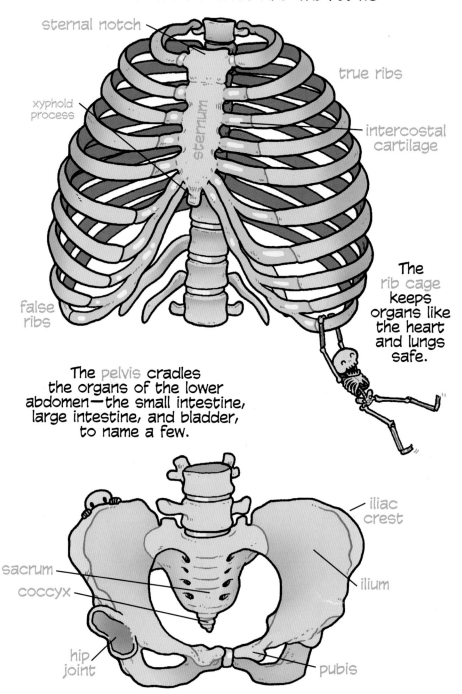

sternal notch

true ribs

xyphoid process

sternum

intercostal cartilage

false ribs

The rib cage keeps organs like the heart and lungs safe.

The pelvis cradles the organs of the lower abdomen—the small intestine, large intestine, and bladder, to name a few.

iliac crest

sacrum

coccyx

ilium

hip joint

pubis

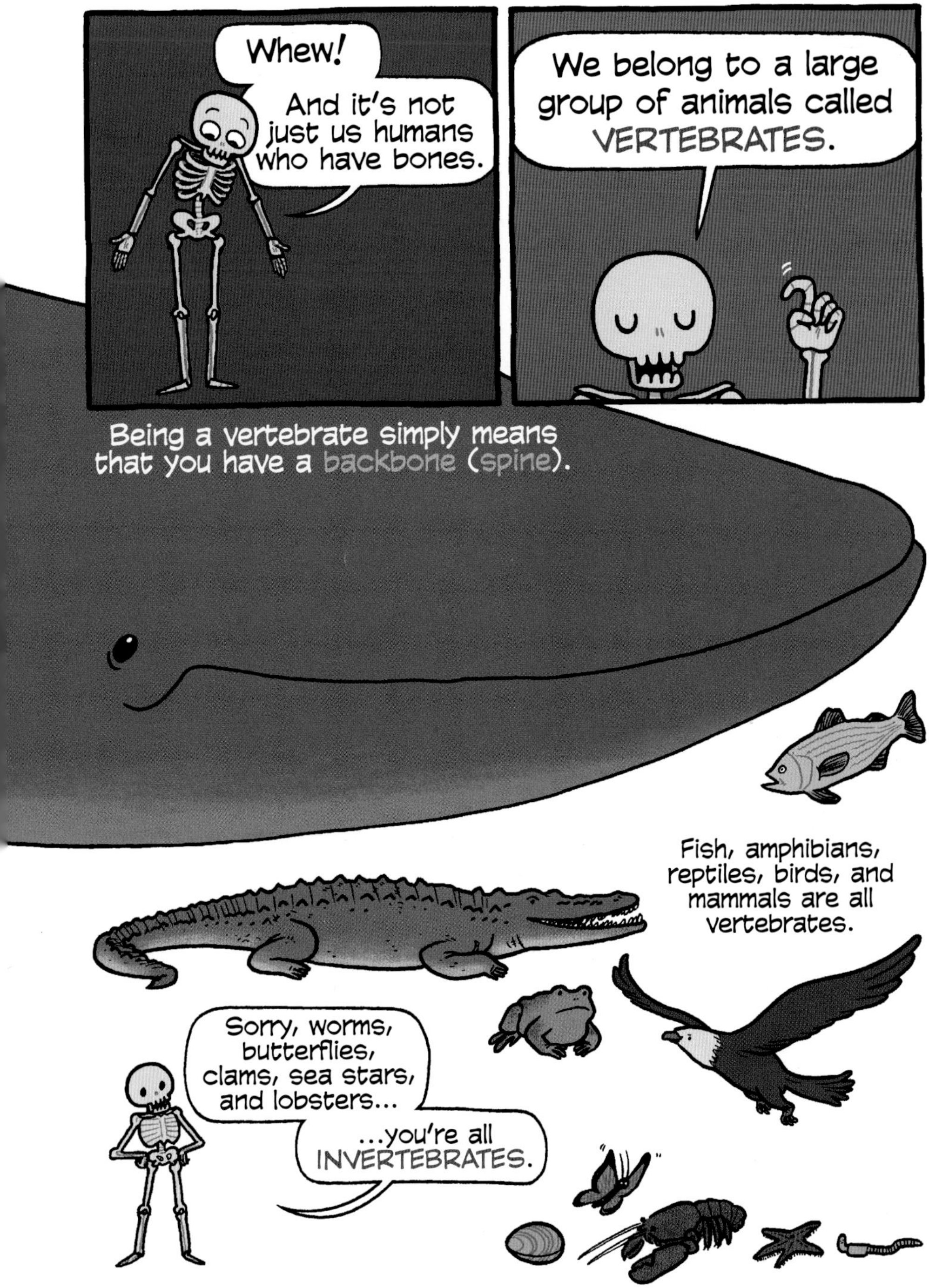
Whew!
And it's not just us humans who have bones.
We belong to a large group of animals called VERTEBRATES.
Being a vertebrate simply means that you have a backbone (spine).
Fish, amphibians, reptiles, birds, and mammals are all vertebrates.
Sorry, worms, butterflies, clams, sea stars, and lobsters...
...you're all INVERTEBRATES.

So far, we've only seen the outside of bones.

Although bones appear to be hard and solid, a closer look will reveal their true nature.

LOOKING INSIDE: BONES

I'm a bone cell!

periosteum (bone sheath)

compact bone

spongy bone

marrow

blood vessels

We're a pretty solid team...

...but there's always a little wiggle room.

Ca

P

Fibers of COLLAGEN— a protein found in the skin and joints— give bones some flexibility, while the elements CALCIUM and PHOSPHOROUS make bones rigid.

In the center of the bone, MARROW produces red blood cells.

You'll see lots of me later!

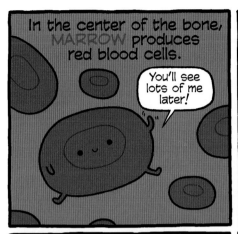

Marrow, along with the COMPACT BONE, acts as a mineral reserve.

EXTRA CALCIUM

EXTRA PHOS-PHOROUS

EXTRA CALCIUM

If certain nutrients in your body are gone or low, they can be taken out of storage in the bone and sent where they're needed.

EXTRA CALCIUM

The vitamins and minerals that strengthen our bones must first get into our bodies!

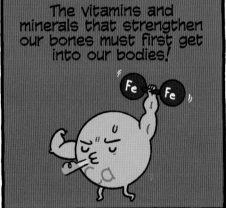

Fe Fe

CALCIUM (from foods like dairy products, fortified juice, and broccoli) and VITAMIN D (from the sun) help to keep bones healthy and strong.

FORTIFIED moo JUICE

These nutrients are especially important when we are growing up.

Speaking of growing up...

FOOSH

...I think it's photo album time!

PHOTO ALBUM

Awwww...
Here's me as a newborn baby. Aren't I the cutest?

We're actually born with over 300 bones, most of which are soft and flexible cartilage.

As we grow, our bones begin to harden with the help of calcium in our diet.

Some bones even fuse together...Remember all those separate bones that make up the skull?

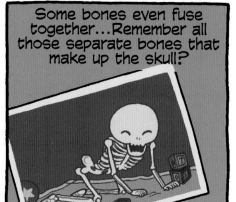

School picture day! I had just lost my front tooth.

Oh! That's me when I was 9. I broke my arm that summer...

As you are probably aware, bones can break.

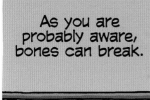

Especially when you are not so good at the monkey bars.

It hurt a bunch when I broke my arm...

CRACK

...but after a few months, my arm healed.

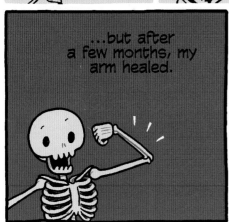

Let's take a look at how bones are able to heal when they break.

yes, please.

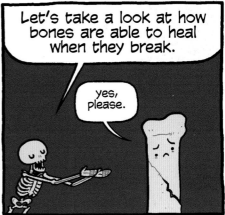

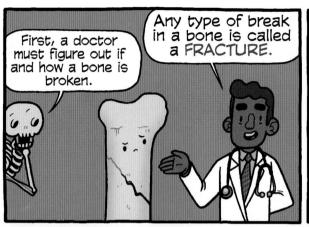

First, a doctor must figure out if and how a bone is broken.

Any type of break in a bone is called a FRACTURE.

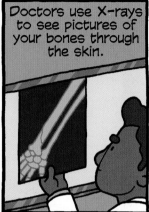

Doctors use X-rays to see pictures of your bones through the skin.

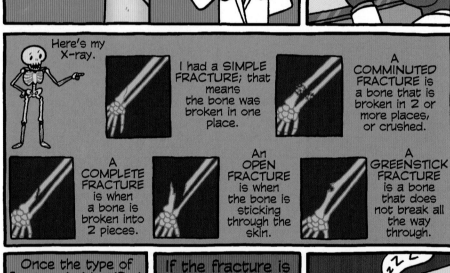

Here's my X-ray.

I had a SIMPLE FRACTURE; that means the bone was broken in one place.

A COMMINUTED FRACTURE is a bone that is broken in 2 or more places, or crushed.

A COMPLETE FRACTURE is when a bone is broken into 2 pieces.

An OPEN FRACTURE is when the bone is sticking through the skin.

A GREENSTICK FRACTURE is a bone that does not break all the way through.

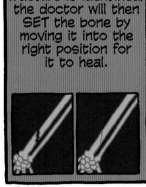

Once the type of fracture is identified, the doctor will then SET the bone by moving it into the right position for it to heal.

If the fracture is in a larger bone (like the femur), or comminuted...

...metal plates or pins can be used to keep the bone from moving around.

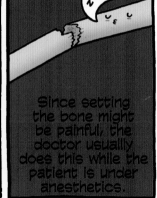

Since setting the bone might be painful, the doctor usually does this while the patient is under anesthetics.

26

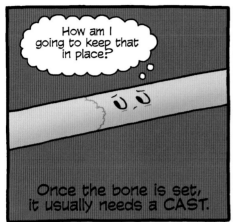

How am I going to keep that in place?

Once the bone is set, it usually needs a CAST.

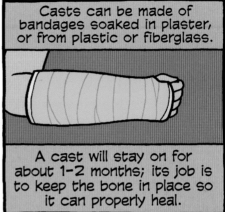

Casts can be made of bandages soaked in plaster, or from plastic or fiberglass.

A cast will stay on for about 1-2 months; its job is to keep the bone in place so it can properly heal.

During this time, new bone cells and blood vessels are made, slowly rebuilding the bone.

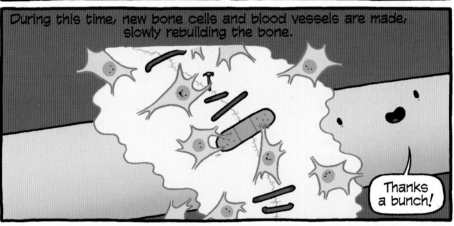

Thanks a bunch!

When the bone is healed, the cast is cut off with a saw.

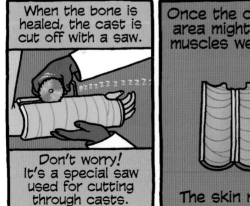

Don't worry! It's a special saw used for cutting through casts.

Once the cast is removed, the injured area might be smaller because those muscles weren't getting any exercise under there.

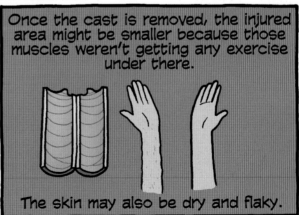

The skin may also be dry and flaky.

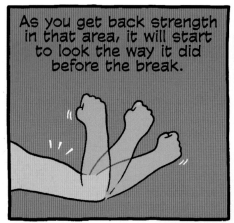

As you get back strength in that area, it will start to look the way it did before the break.

I might even have you do special exercises to help the injured area get strong again.

This is called PHYSICAL THERAPY.

Broken bones can happen to anyone: big or small, young or old.

Here are some things you can do to help keep your bones happy, healthy, and safe.

Remember those bone-healthy foods?

Eat us!

Regular exercise will keep bones strong.

Protective gear—like helmets and knee pads—will help keep your bones safe, too!

I got this!

There are more pieces to the skeletal puzzle:

How are all of our bones connected?

JOINTS!

A JOINT is the place where two bones meet. All 206 bones in the human body are linked together by joints.

FIXED JOINTS are set in place and do not move. See those squiggly lines? Those are fixed joints called SUTURES.

Doin' the twist!

CARTILAGINOUS JOINTS are slightly moveable. When I twist my spine, these discs of cartilage help it rotate.

MOVABLE JOINTS do just that— they move! Sometimes these joints are called SYNOVIAL JOINTS, because moveable joints are filled with SYNOVIAL FLUID.

I help reduce friction when joints move.

These joints can be found all over the body, and there are a few different types:

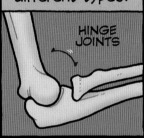

HINGE JOINTS

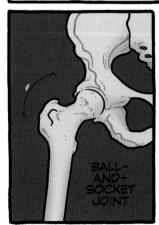

BALL-AND-SOCKET JOINT

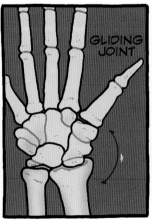

GLIDING JOINT

To top it all off, tough pieces of elastic tissue called LIGAMENTS connect bone to bone, strengthening each joint.

Sometimes our joints make a "cracking" or "popping" sound when they are bent. Here's how!

The synovial fluid inside the joints contains nutrients for cells to keep the cartilage healthy.

The fluid also contains gases like CARBON DIOXIDE and OXYGEN.

People think that when a joint is bent, more gas gets into the fluid, making gas bubbles. These bubbles "pop," and that's the sound you hear!

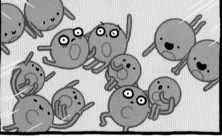

Scientists are still researching why our joints crack.

What they do know is that cracking your joints does not cause arthritis or serious damage—you just shouldn't do it all the time.

Okay, so we've got BONE CELLS...

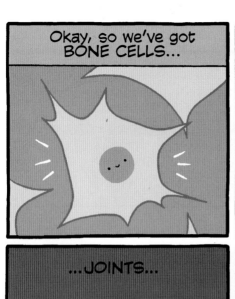

...BONES...

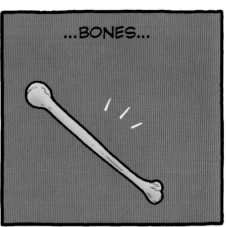

...JOINTS...

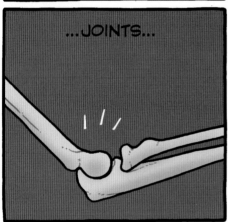

...and LIGAMENTS.

Well, that about wraps it up for the skeletal system.

It's time for me to change into my costume for...

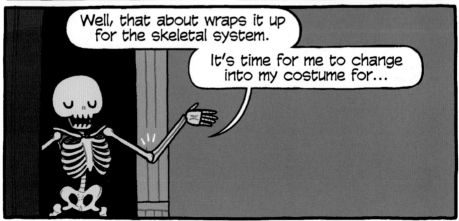

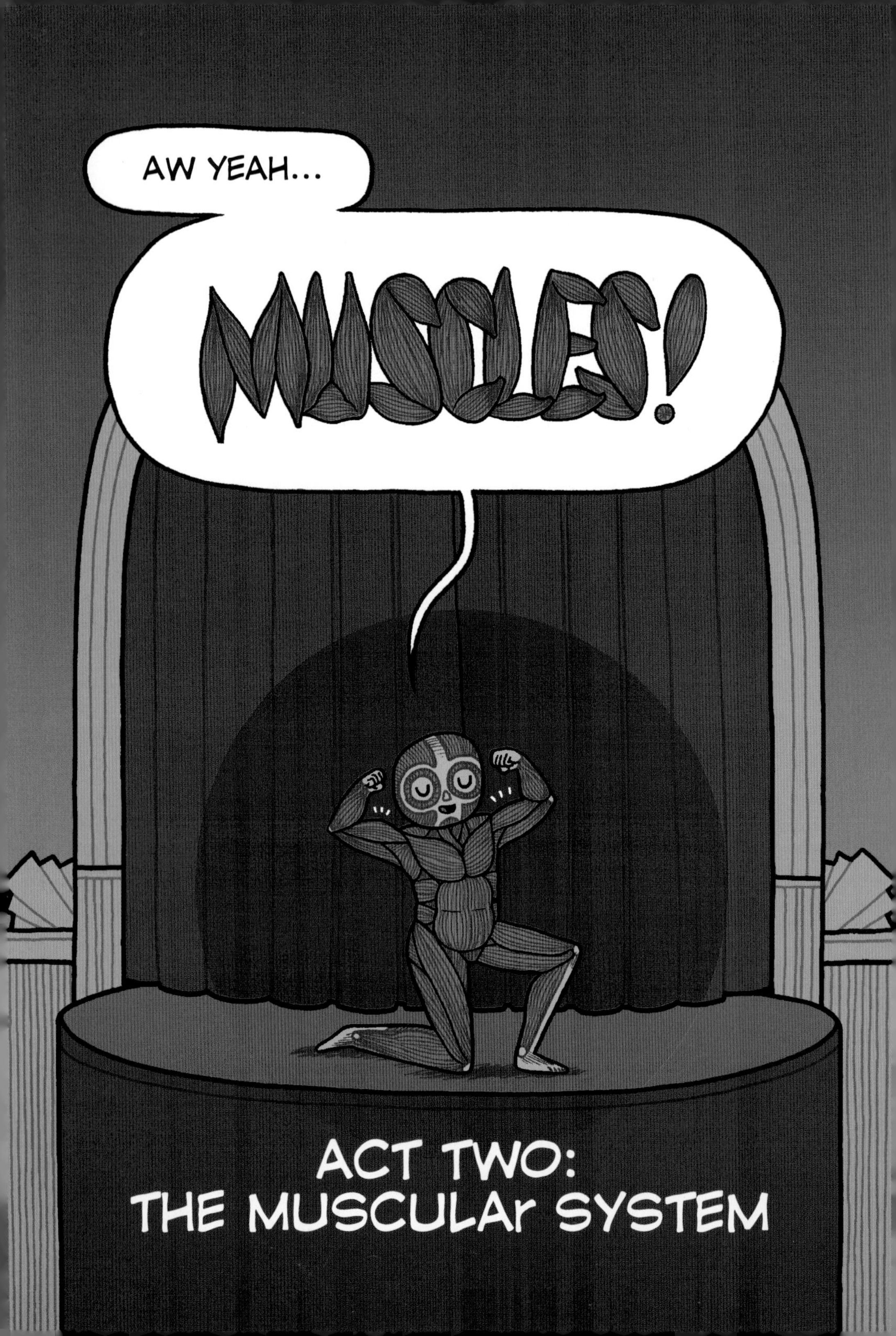
AW YEAH...
MUSCLES!
ACT TWO:
THE MUSCULAr SYSTEM

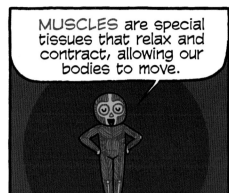

MUSCLES are special tissues that relax and contract, allowing our bodies to move.

The human body has more than 640 SKELETAL MUSCLES responsible for all this movin' and shakin'.

And there are even more muscles on the inside...

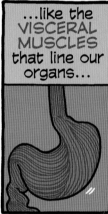

...like the VISCERAL MUSCLES that line our organs...

...and the CARDIAC MUSCLES that help our heart beat.

But let's talk about those skeletal muscles first.

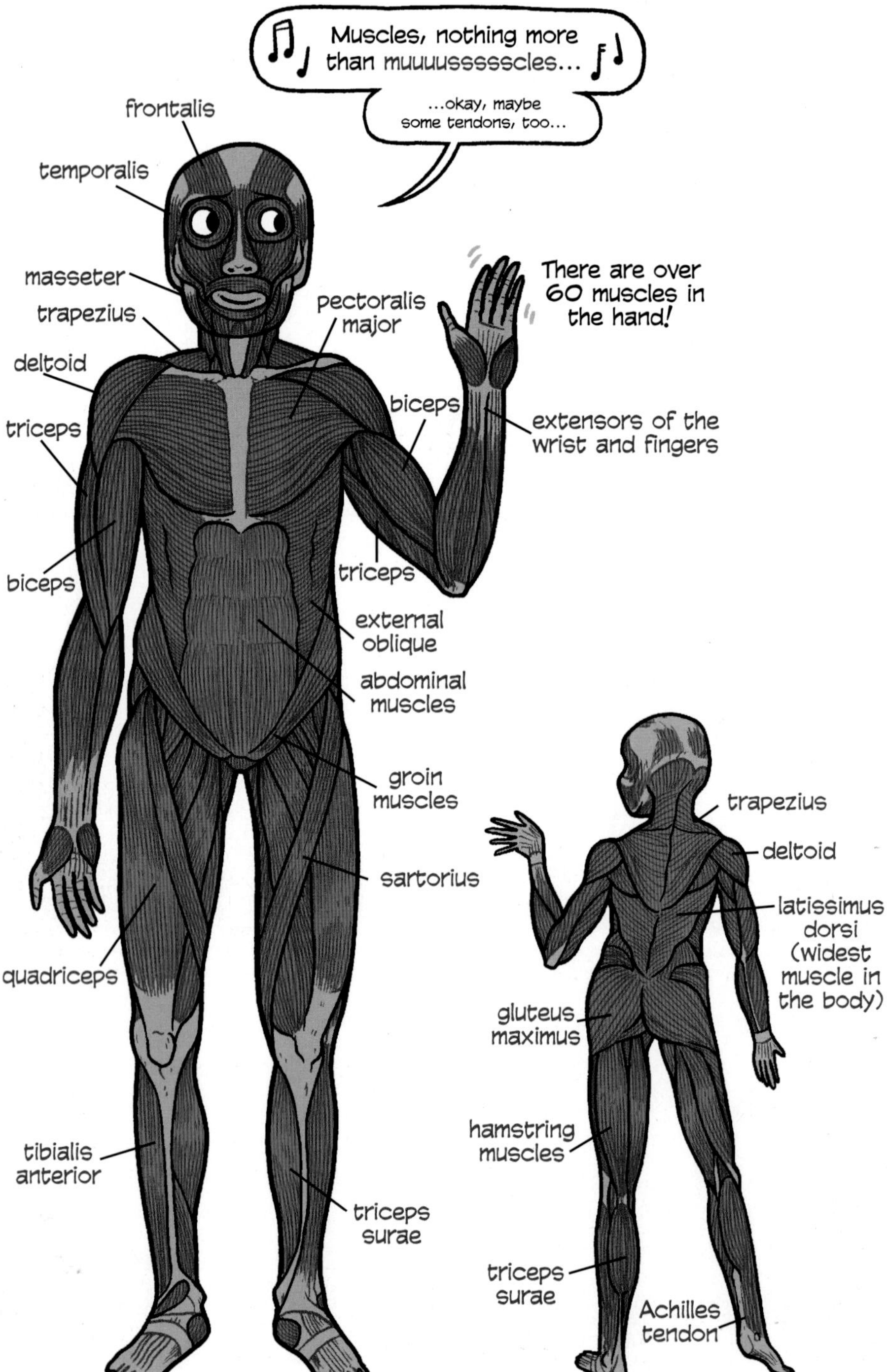

Muscles, nothing more than muuuussssscles...
...okay, maybe some tendons, too...
There are over 60 muscles in the hand!
frontalis
temporalis
masseter
trapezius
deltoid
triceps
biceps
pectoralis major
biceps
extensors of the wrist and fingers
triceps
external oblique
abdominal muscles
groin muscles
sartorius
quadriceps
tibialis anterior
triceps surae
trapezius
deltoid
latissimus dorsi (widest muscle in the body)
gluteus maximus
hamstring muscles
triceps surae
Achilles tendon

The MASSETER is the strongest muscle.

With all the muscles of the jaw working together, our molars (back teeth) can chomp down with a force of 200 pounds.

So when we chew, our molars are coming down on the food with the force of 20 bowling balls!

In the face there are about 40 muscles.

They work together to give us a whole lot of facial expressions.

The TONGUE is a muscle, too, and it never rests.

Even as we sleep, the tongue pushes saliva to the back of the throat to be swallowed.

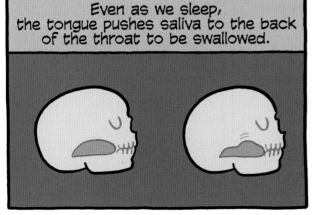

I can't catch a break!

Luckily for most of the skeletal muscles, they work together in pairs.

640 divided by 2 is 320 pairs!

Say you need to bend your elbow...

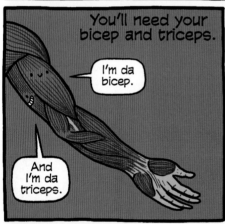

You'll need your bicep and triceps.

I'm da bicep.

And I'm da triceps.

Your bicep CONTRACTS, pulling your forearm up.

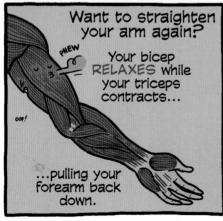

Want to straighten your arm again?

Your bicep RELAXES while your triceps contracts...

PHEW

OOF!

...pulling your forearm back down.

GO TEAM MUSCLE!!

MU   MU

When muscles move, they may look larger or smaller, but they are simply changing shape.

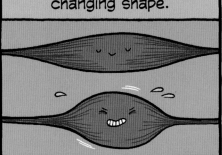

However, exercise can strengthen muscles over time, and that might make them bigger.

Let's see what goes on inside a skeletal muscle...

LOOKING INSIDE: SKELETAL MUSCLE

Skeletal muscles are bundles of, well, bundles. Each muscle contains bundles of smaller muscle fibers, and those bundles contain the even smaller muscle cells.

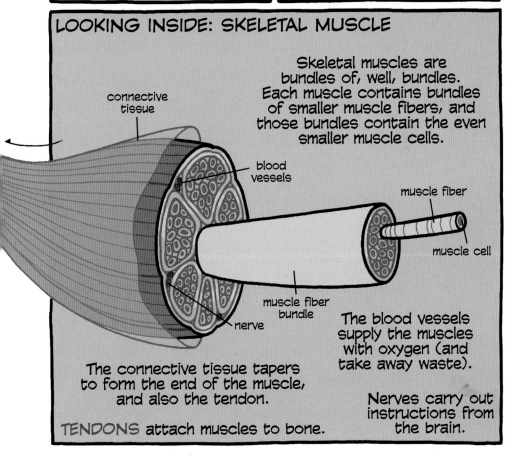

connective tissue

blood vessels

muscle fiber

muscle cell

muscle fiber bundle

nerve

The connective tissue tapers to form the end of the muscle, and also the tendon.

TENDONS attach muscles to bone.

The blood vessels supply the muscles with oxygen (and take away waste).

Nerves carry out instructions from the brain.

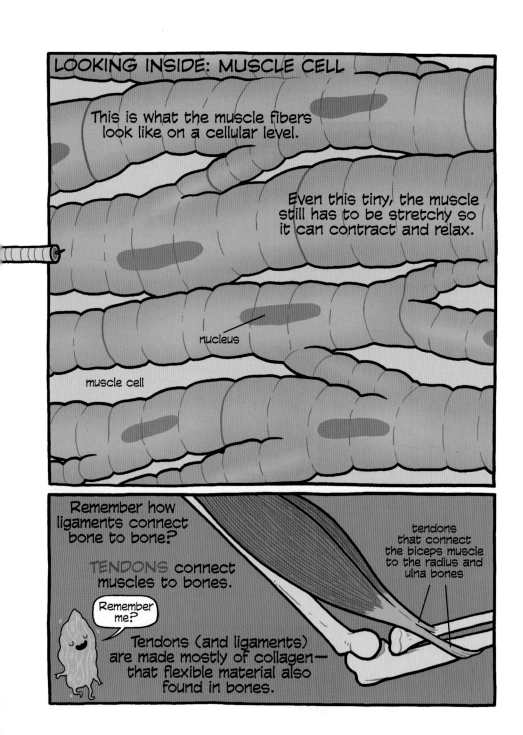

LOOKING INSIDE: MUSCLE CELL

This is what the muscle fibers look like on a cellular level.

Even this tiny, the muscle still has to be stretchy so it can contract and relax.

nucleus

muscle cell

Remember how ligaments connect bone to bone?

TENDONS connect muscles to bones.

Remember me?

Tendons (and ligaments) are made mostly of collagen—that flexible material also found in bones.

tendons that connect the biceps muscle to the radius and ulna bones

Just as we've seen with bones, muscles can get injured, too.

Oof—I've got a sore shoulder.

A STRAIN happens when a muscle is stretched too far. This is common in the neck, back, and legs, especially after lots of exercise or when playing a new sport.

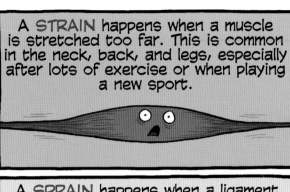

A SPRAIN happens when a ligament is overstretched or torn. This will usually hurt right after the injury and there may be bruising or swelling around the sprain.

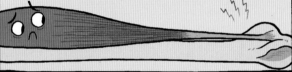

Both strains and sprains need rest to heal. A sprain might also need a splint, a cast, or a bandage.

R. I. C. E.

A doctor or coach might recommend that you R.I.C.E. your injury. This stands for: Rest, Ice, Compression, and Elevation.

Most of the time, a strain will take about 1 week to heal, while a sprain may take 3–4 weeks to heal.

"Warming up" and "cooling down" before and after any exercise is a good way to aviod strains, sprains, and sore muscles.

Here are a few ways to stretch some important muscle groups:

This stretch extends the lower back muscles and hamstrings (and you don't have to worry about balancing, because you are lying down!).

The calves, back, and hamstrings (again) all benefit from this stretch...

...while this stretch extends the quadreceps.

Pulling your arm toward you will stretch the deltoid and shoulder muscles.

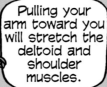

This is another stretch that works your back muscles.

It's good to stretch your back. It might not seem like it works very hard, but those muscles are working ALL the time, helping you stand and sit up.

Including light exercise in your stretching routine is good, too! Try a little jogging in place or doing jumping jacks.

Now that I'm all warmed up, let's talk about muscle function.

phew!

You might have heard this question at Thanksgiving: "White meat or dark meat?"

When we eat animals—like turkey, beef, fish, etc.—we mostly eat the muscles.

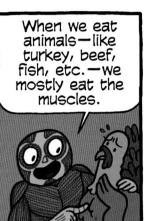

Even though our skeletal muscles all move the same way, some have different jobs when it comes to movement.

Some muscles are better for quick bursts of movement—like sprinting.

Some muscles are better over long periods of exercise—like walking.

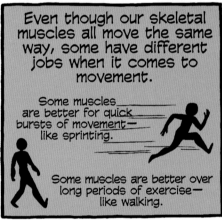

In a turkey, the pectoral muscles (white meat) are good for short bursts of intense movement—like flying.

And the thigh muscles (dark meat) are used for everyday low-endurance movement—like walking.

Humans are the same way—our pectorals and thigh muscles do the same kind of things the turkey's do.*

Just don't eat me!

Or me!

Sometimes, when you are growing, your muscles might hurt for what seems like no reason.

I don't get it—I stretched!

*Except, you know, humans can't fly.

41

These are called "growing pains."

Not all kids get growing pains, but those who do usually get them from ages 3-5 or 8-12.

Growing pains are caused, in part, by growing, but not the way you might think.*

At night, your body is hard at work, especially as you grow.

z

That is why growing pains strike at night.

They often feel like aches and pains in the legs — in the thighs, in the calves, or behind the knees.

The good news is that growing pains go away by morning.

Aaaah.

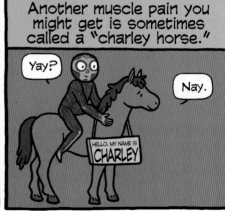

Another muscle pain you might get is sometimes called a "charley horse."

Yay?

Nay.

HELLO, MY NAME IS CHARLEY

*Hormones are actually responsible for those pesky growing pains, but we'll get to them in the endocrine system.

A "charley horse" is actually a nickname for a muscle SPASM or CRAMP, an involuntary contraction of 2 or more muscles.

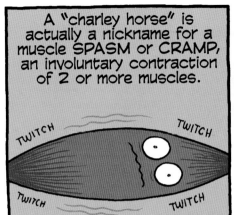

TWITCH TWITCH TWITCH TWITCH

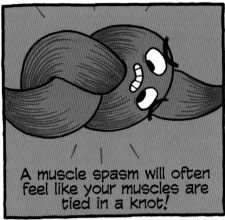

A muscle spasm will often feel like your muscles are tied in a knot!

YEEOW!!

Possible causes include overexercise, not stretching before and/or after exercise, dehydration, and salt imbalance.

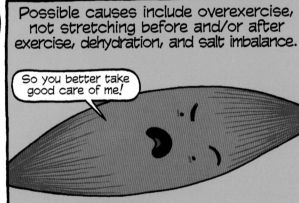

So you better take good care of me!

If you remember to stretch every day and drink plenty of water, you should be able to avoid charley horses.

HELLO, MY NAME IS CHARLEY

Well, excuuuuuse me.

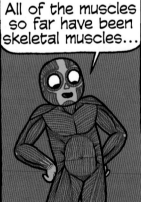

All of the muscles so far have been skeletal muscles...

...and skeletal muscles are all VOLUNTARY MUSCLES.

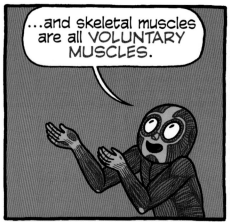

That means that they need the brain to tell them to—

CONTRACT!

RELAX!

But there are 2 other types of muscles and they are both INVOLUNTARY MUSCLES.

C'est la vie!

That means they work without you having to think about it...

...even though involuntary muscles are still monitored by the brain.

Aw, c'mon. I want a vacation.

These 2 types of muscles are...

CARDIAC MUSCLE!

Mmm-hmm.

Found only in the heart, cardiac muscle is what makes your heart beat.

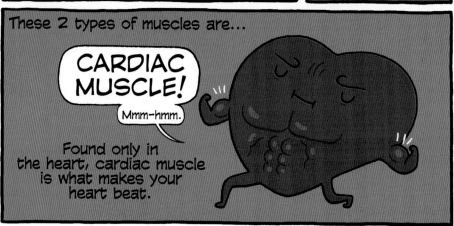

VISCERAL MUSCLES!

These muscles are found in the intestines and abdominal organs.

When your stomach moves food around, it's using the visceral muscles in the stomach.

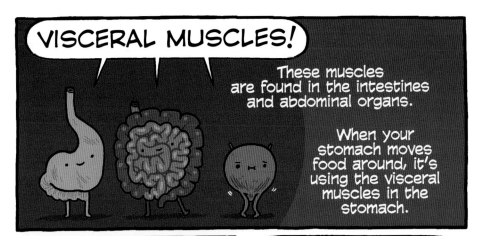

All muscles are fueled, in part, by OXYGEN.

Reporting for duty!

This is why we ::huff huff:: need to breathe more during ::huff huff:: exercise.

huff huff
huff huff

So, when the musculatory system is working hard to move the body, where do we get that oxygen to do all that movin' and shakin'?

ACT THREE:
THE RESPIRATORY SYSTEM

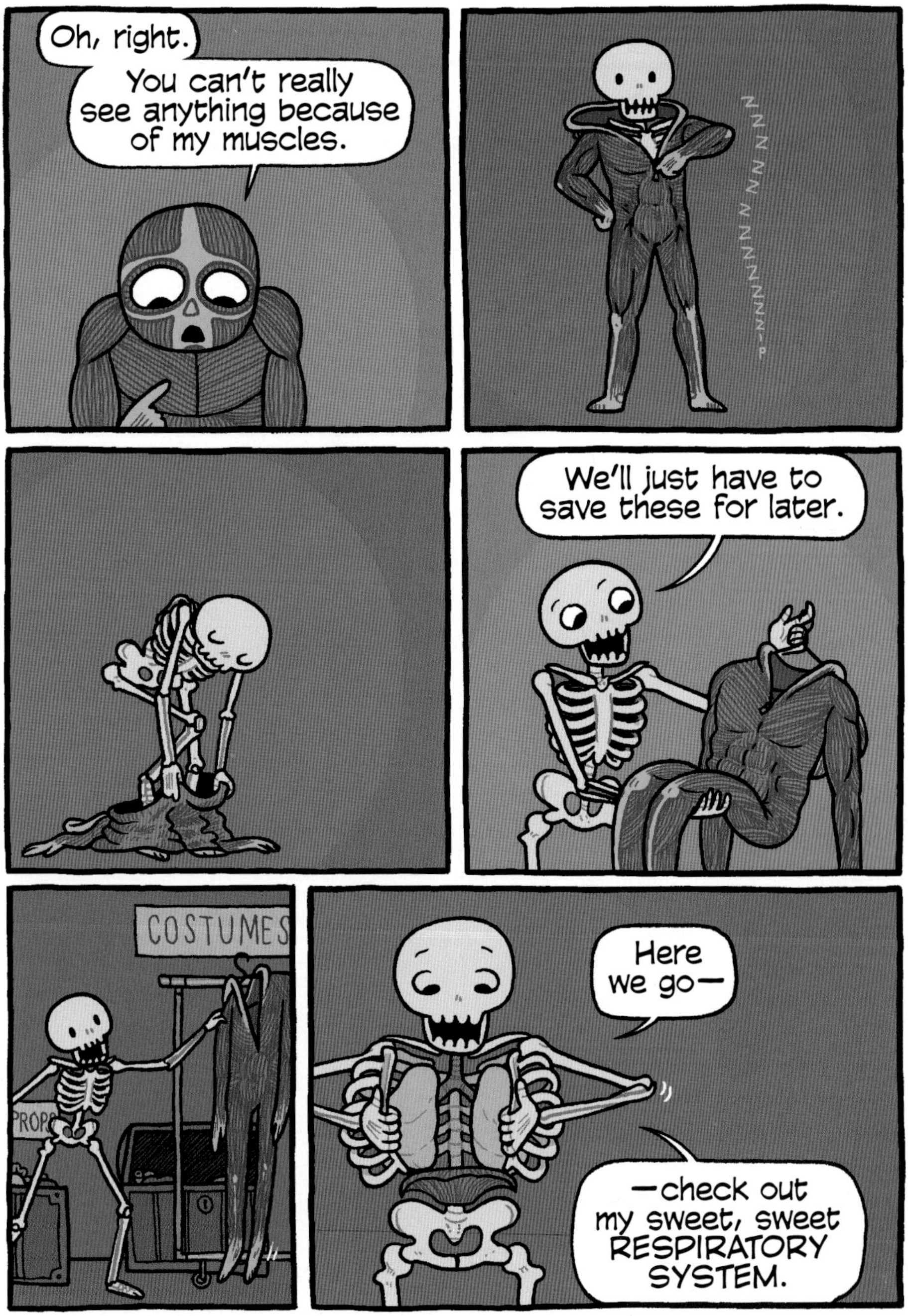
Oh, right.
You can't really see anything because of my muscles.
ZZZZZZZZZZZZZZZZIP
We'll just have to save these for later.
COSTUMES
PROPS
Here we go—
—check out my sweet, sweet RESPIRATORY SYSTEM.

Thanks, rib cage, for keeping it safe.

Almost every living thing on this planet needs OXYGEN to survive...

...and human beings are no exception.

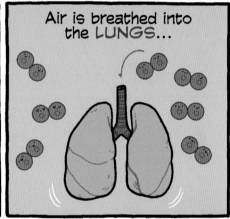

Air is breathed into the LUNGS...

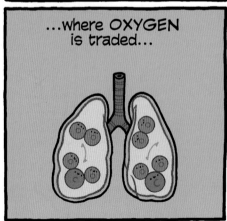

...where OXYGEN is traded...

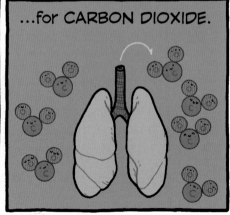

...for CARBON DIOXIDE.

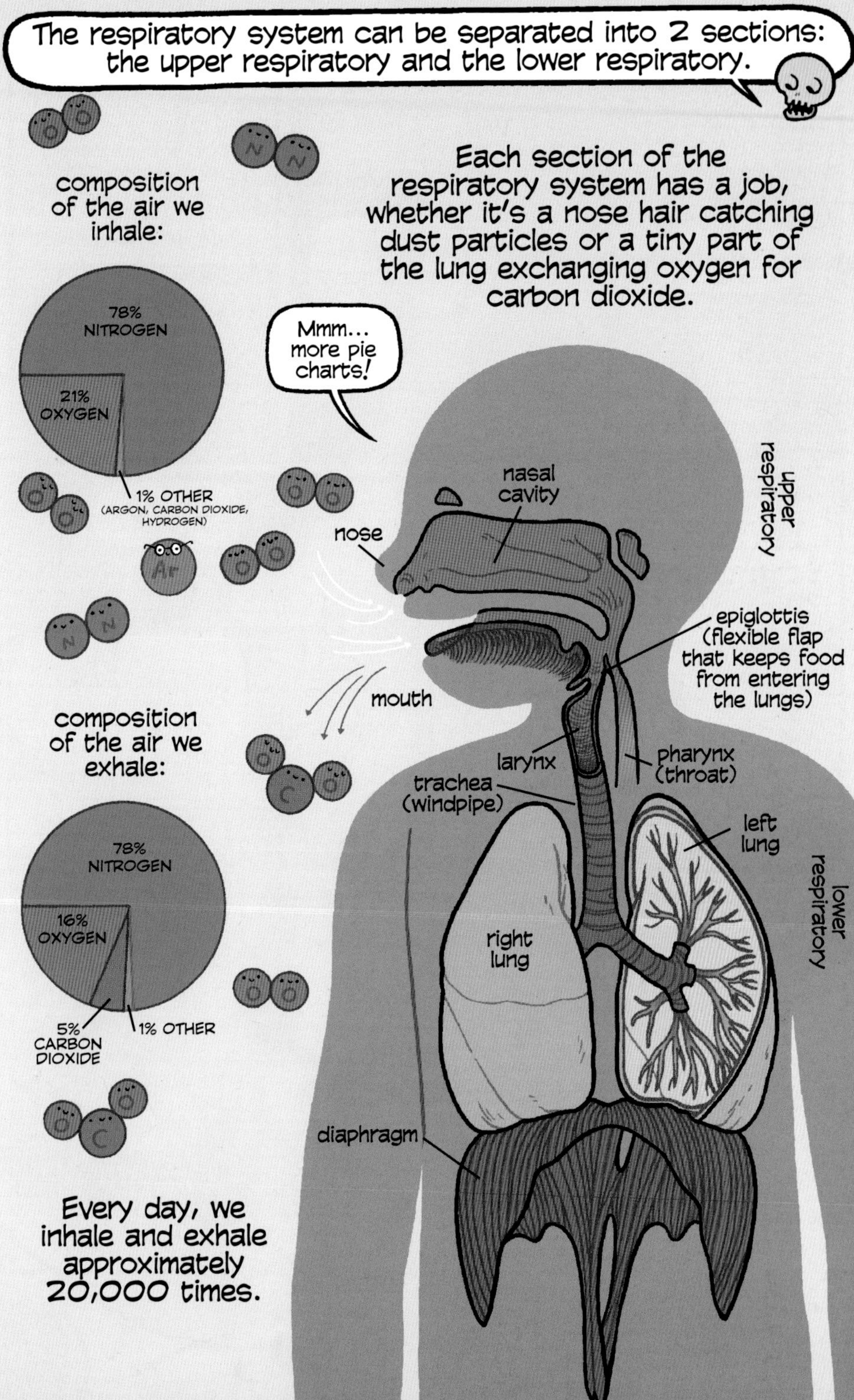
The respiratory system can be separated into 2 sections: the upper respiratory and the lower respiratory.
Each section of the respiratory system has a job, whether it's a nose hair catching dust particles or a tiny part of the lung exchanging oxygen for carbon dioxide.
composition of the air we inhale:
78% NITROGEN
21% OXYGEN
1% OTHER (ARGON, CARBON DIOXIDE, HYDROGEN)
Mmm... more pie charts!
composition of the air we exhale:
78% NITROGEN
16% OXYGEN
5% CARBON DIOXIDE
1% OTHER
nasal cavity
nose
upper respiratory
epiglottis (flexible flap that keeps food from entering the lungs)
mouth
larynx
pharynx (throat)
trachea (windpipe)
left lung
lower respiratory
right lung
diaphragm
Every day, we inhale and exhale approximately 20,000 times.

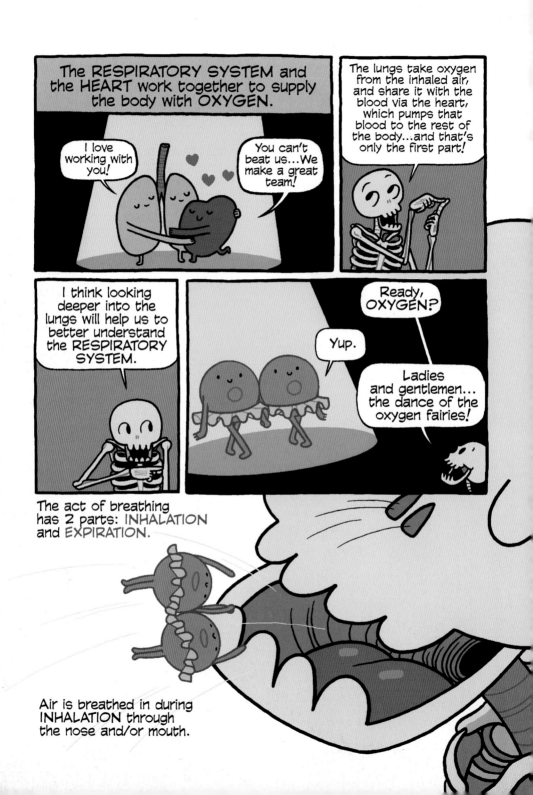

The RESPIRATORY SYSTEM and the HEART work together to supply the body with OXYGEN.

I love working with you!

You can't beat us...We make a great team!

The lungs take oxygen from the inhaled air, and share it with the blood via the heart, which pumps that blood to the rest of the body...and that's only the first part!

I think looking deeper into the lungs will help us to better understand the RESPIRATORY SYSTEM.

Ready, OXYGEN?

Yup.

Ladies and gentlemen... the dance of the oxygen fairies!

The act of breathing has 2 parts: INHALATION and EXPIRATION.

Air is breathed in during INHALATION through the nose and/or mouth.

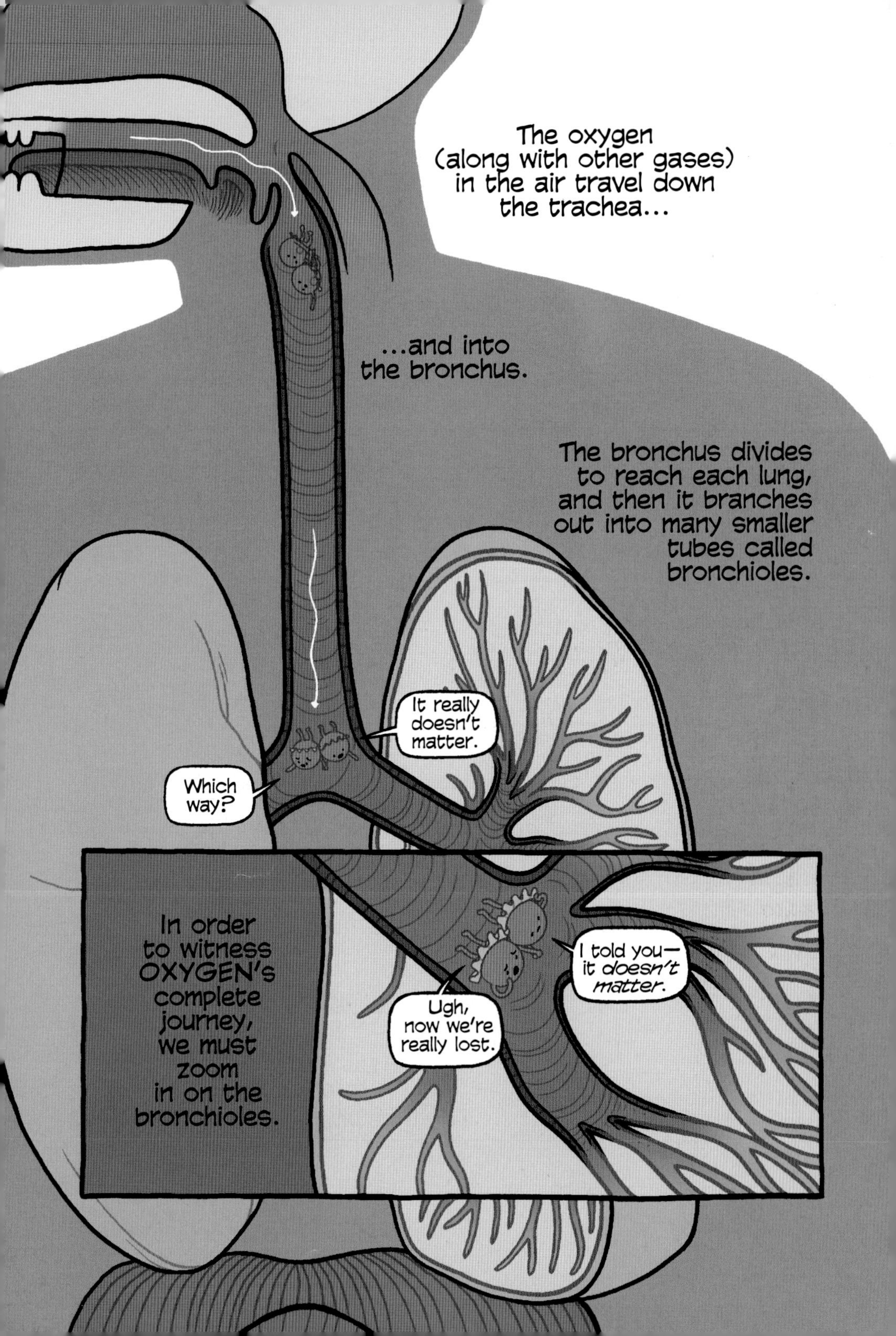

The oxygen (along with other gases) in the air travel down the trachea...
...and into the bronchus.
The bronchus divides to reach each lung, and then it branches out into many smaller tubes called bronchioles.
Which way?
It really doesn't matter.
In order to witness OXYGEN's complete journey, we must zoom in on the bronchioles.
Ugh, now we're really lost.
I told you—it *doesn't matter*.

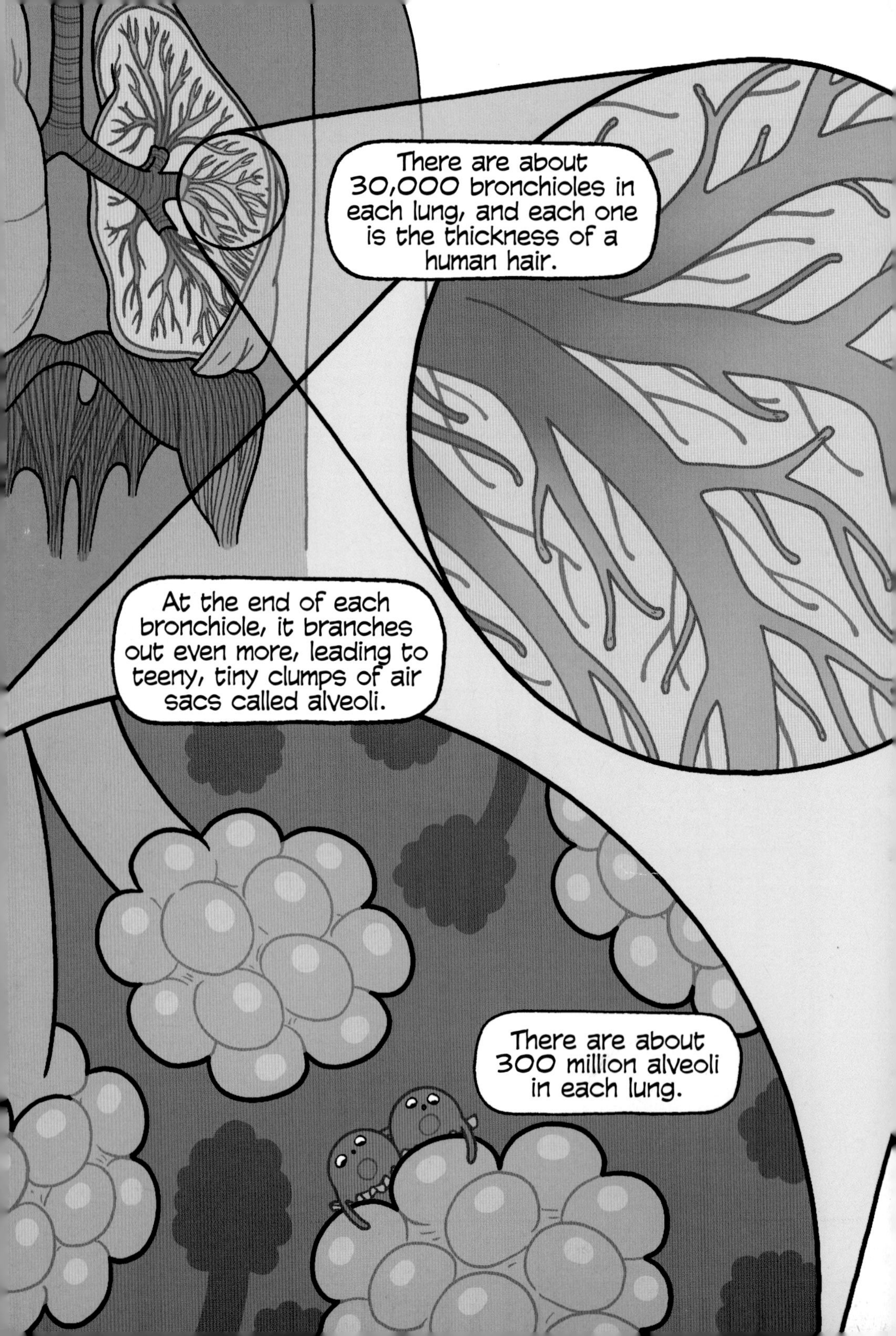
There are about 30,000 bronchioles in each lung, and each one is the thickness of a human hair.
At the end of each bronchiole, it branches out even more, leading to teeny, tiny clumps of air sacs called alveoli.
There are about 300 million alveoli in each lung.

Each alveoli is covered in a mesh of very small blood vessels (capillaries).

Shall we?

Yes, please!

Once the oxygen from the air we inhaled reaches the alveoli, GAS EXCHANGE takes place. Time to zoom in even further...

LOOKING INSIDE: GAS EXCHANGE

Our bodies need that oxygen to survive. So, through the thin walls of the capillaries, a trade is made:

RED BLOOD CELLS drop off CARBON DIOXIDE and other wastes from the body in exchange for fresh new OXYGEN.

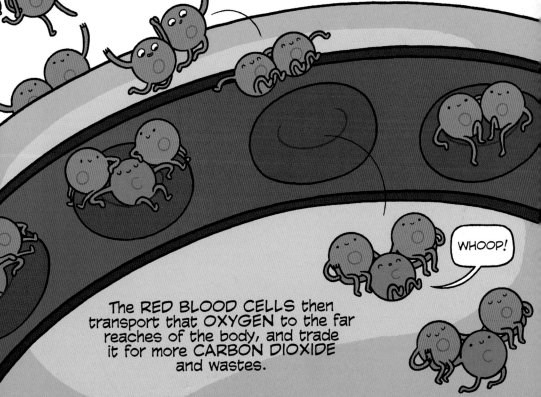

WHOOP!

The RED BLOOD CELLS then transport that OXYGEN to the far reaches of the body, and trade it for more CARBON DIOXIDE and wastes.

OXYGEN reaches every single cell...

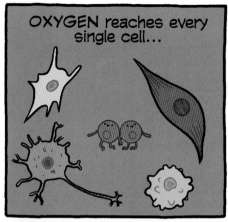

After all, we want to keep our "stagehands" happy and healthy.

Once the gas exchange is made in the lungs, we need to get those wastes out of the body—

Get me outta here!

—and that's when EXPIRATION happens.

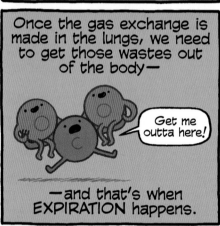

With a little help from the diaphragm, our lungs EXHALE the "stale" air.

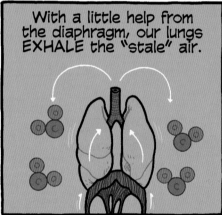

All this happens much faster than it took to read the last few pages.

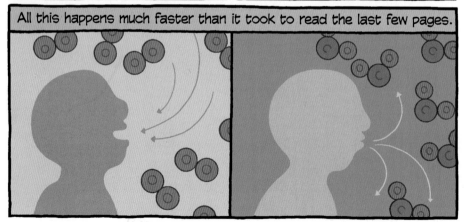

Let's chat a bit about AIR.

It's not just us, you know...

H₂ (HYDROGEN)

He₂ (HELIUM)

CO₂ (CARBON DIOXIDE)

N₂ (NITROGEN)

O₂ (OXYGEN)

That's right! The air we breathe is only 21% OXYGEN.

Other gases make up the rest.

Our bodies produce CARBON DIOXIDE, but we need OXYGEN... So where does all this OXYGEN come from?

The world's supply of OXYGEN comes from plants and algae.

Plants and algae take in CARBON DIOXIDE to use as food...

...and expel OXYGEN as waste!

Did you know that trees are NOT the world's biggest producer of OXYGEN?

Wait, whaaaaat?

7 out of every 10 breaths that you take use OXYGEN from itty-bitty ocean plants called PHYTOPLANKTON.

So next time the ocean waves, wave back. Because you owe it your LIFE.

Aaah, air.

POK!

To breathe, or not to breathe...

...it's not really a question, is it?

We talked earlier about muscle movement being VOLUNTARY or INVOLUNTARY, but actions can have these titles as well.

Throwing a ball, writing, and jumping are all VOLUNTARY actions...

JUMPING!

DIGESTING!

...but salivating, digesting, and sweating are all INVOLUNTARY actions.

BREATHING is an involuntary action; your body breathes on its own without you having to tell it to.

Let's take a look at an involuntary action that has to do with breathing: the...

YAWN

A YAWN is a deep breath that gets more air into the lungs.

In fact, if you try to think about breathing, it's harder to breathe. Try it!

56

Yawning is contagious—if you see someone yawn, it can trigger a yawn for you. Even reading about yawns can make you yawn! (Have you yawned yet?)

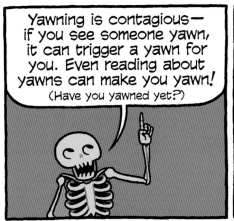

So here's what is weird: we don't really know WHY we yawn.

However, scientists do have some theories* as to why we yawn... Here are a few of the more popular ones:

#1. Yawns are triggered when the body needs more oxygen (or has too much carbon dioxide).

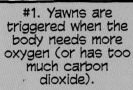

This theory has been tested, and it does not seem to hold up in experiments.

#2. Yawns are a signal to others that you are bored or tired.

Uh, am I boring you?

Humans use body language to communicate many things, and maybe yawns are part of the vocabulary.

#3. Yawns are your body's way of stretching your jaw, lungs, and upper body muscles.

Stretching helps to increase circulation and can make you feel more awake.

Regardless of WHY we yawn, it's certainly not a bad thing.

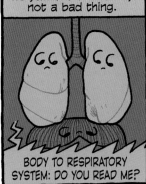

BODY TO RESPIRATORY SYSTEM: DO YOU READ ME?

WE NEED A YAWN—NOW!

Sure thang!!

Yeah—we got this!

Now, if you're looking for some one to blame for the hiccups...

HIC!

*theory: an idea or set of ideas that is intended to explain facts or events

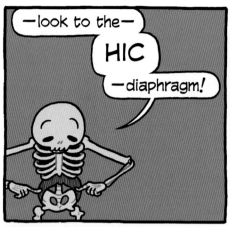

−look to the−

HIC

−diaphragm!

Hey! I just helped you out with that yawn!

The diaphragm is a dome-shaped muscle below the lungs that helps us to inhale and exhale.

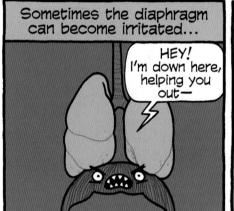

Sometimes the diaphragm can become irritated...

HEY! I'm down here, helping you out−

...causing it to spasm.

−and I don't appreciate you blaming me−

HIC

This quick contraction−

HIC

−makes us suck air into our lungs very−

HIC

−quickly, creating that classic "HICCUP" sound−

HIC

BOO!

Hey! My hiccups−

−they're gone!

Thanks!

Getting anything other than air into your lungs can be very dangerous.

So, our bodies have a lot of ways to keep things like dirt, dust, and germs from getting in.

Nose hairs, snot (aka mucus), and tiny hairlike cilia in the trachea all help trap foreign particles before they reach the lungs.

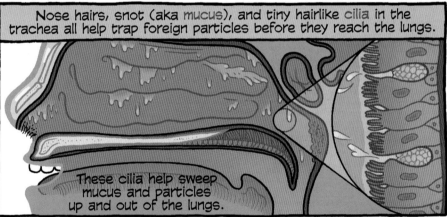

These cilia help sweep mucus and particles up and out of the lungs.

Coughing and sneezing help get out unwanted particles as well.

AAAAH

CHOO

Cigarette smoke is especially damaging—it goes all the way into the lungs and can weaken or even injure them permanently.

HONK!

Every once in a while, something that shouldn't gets into the respiratory system.

Your body responds by using its IMMUNE SYSTEM.

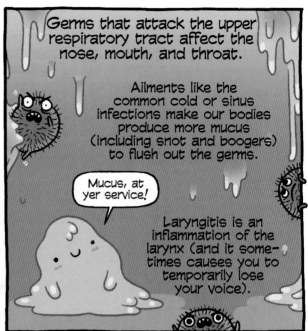

Germs that attack the upper respiratory tract affect the nose, mouth, and throat.

Ailments like the common cold or sinus infections make our bodies produce more mucus (including snot and boogers) to flush out the germs.

Mucus, at yer service!

Laryngitis is an inflammation of the larynx (and it sometimes causes you to temporarily lose your voice).

Infections in the lower respiratory tract (the bronchus and the lungs) are more serious.

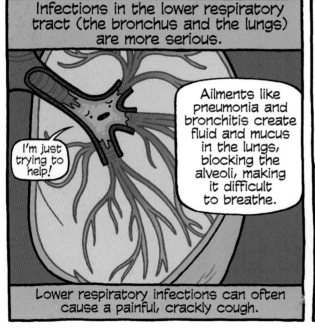

I'm just trying to help!

Ailments like pneumonia and bronchitis create fluid and mucus in the lungs, blocking the alveoli, making it difficult to breathe.

Lower respiratory infections can often cause a painful, crackly cough.

A lot of the time, these infections can be treated by rest, and sometimes with medicine.

But these aren't the only problems that can affect the respiratory system.

Bring out the lungs!

We're going to talk about ASTHMA.

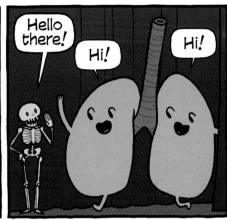

Hello there!

Hi!

Hi!

ASTHMA is a condition that causes trouble in the airway; this includes the bronchus and bronchioles.

An ASTHMA FLARE-UP (sometimes called an asmtha attack) happens when the airway becomes swollen, spasms, and narrows.

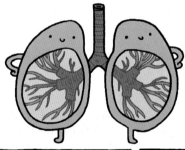

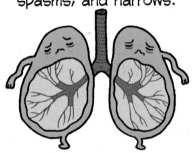

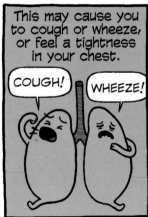

This may cause you to cough or wheeze, or feel a tightness in your chest.

COUGH!

WHEEZE!

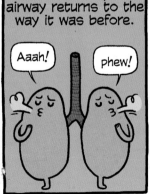

After a flare-up, the airway returns to the way it was before.

Aaah!

phew!

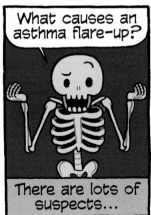

What causes an asthma flare-up?

There are lots of suspects...

...that can trigger an asthma flare-up.

3 IN

2.5 IN

2 IN

DUST

ANIMAL HAIR

MOLD

CIGARETTE SMOKE

perfume

AIR POLLUTION

Even exercise or drastic changes in air temperature can cause a flare-up.

Asthma affects 1-2 out of every 10 kids. Maybe you have asthma—if not, you probably know someone who does.

Okay. You and you will be allergens.

A lot of the time, asthma goes away by the time you reach adulthood.

Asthma runs in families: if your parents or grand-parents had it, you are more likely to have it.

There are a few ways to treat asthma...

That's the one!

That mold caused my flare-up!

Just identifying and avoiding triggers can help to prevent flare-ups.

And there are medicines that help treat asthma.

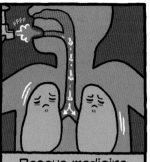

Rescue medicine, usually from an inhaler, is breathed directly into the lungs.

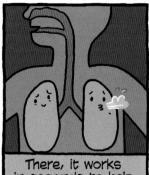

There, it works in seconds to help open the airways during a flare-up.

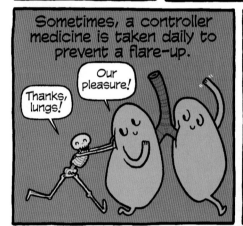

Sometimes, a controller medicine is taken daily to prevent a flare-up.

Thanks, lungs!

Our pleasure!

The respiratory system has shown us that AIR and OXYGEN are not only important but also necessary for humans to live.

But we need that OXYGEN in every nook and cranny...

So how does OXYGEN travel to the far reaches of our bodies?

ACT FOUR: THE CARDIOVASCULAR SYSTEM

Here it is, in all of its gory glory.

There are several parts of our CARDIOVASCULAR SYSTEM making sure that blood gets to where it needs to go.

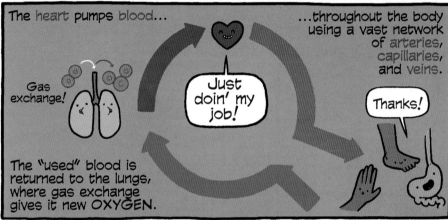

The heart pumps blood...

...throughout the body using a vast network of arteries, capillaries, and veins.

Gas exchange!

Just doin' my job!

Thanks!

The "used" blood is returned to the lungs, where gas exchange gives it new OXYGEN.

Blood is the main method of travel for not just OXYGEN, but also CARBON DIOXIDE, nutrients, and heat.

Hi again!

PROTEIN

SUGAR

SUGAR

Seeing the whole thing will help us understand the cardiovascular system.

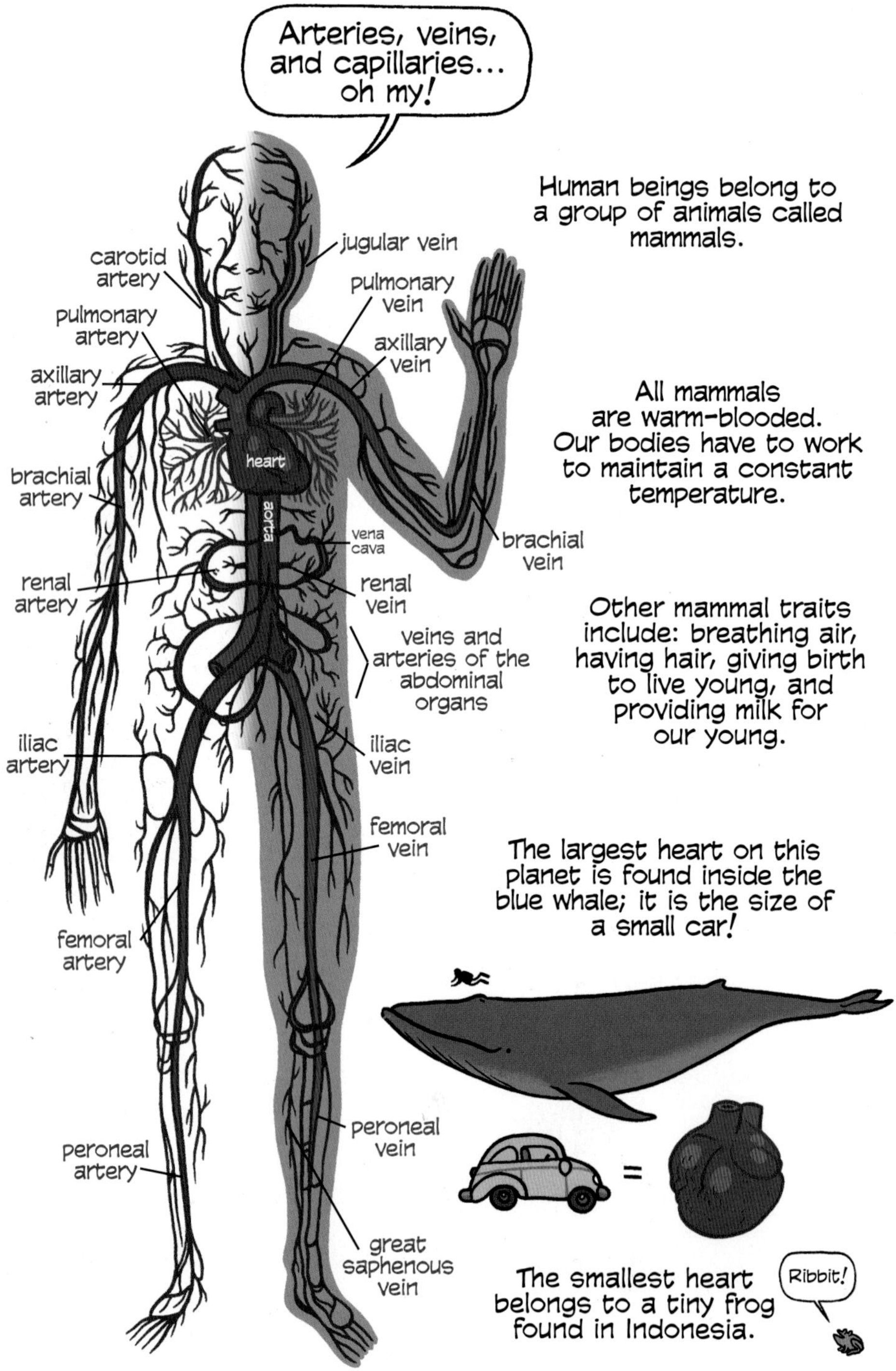

Arteries, veins, and capillaries... oh my!
carotid artery
pulmonary artery
axillary artery
brachial artery
renal artery
iliac artery
femoral artery
peroneal artery
jugular vein
pulmonary vein
axillary vein
heart
aorta
vena cava
brachial vein
renal vein
veins and arteries of the abdominal organs
iliac vein
femoral vein
peroneal vein
great saphenous vein
Human beings belong to a group of animals called mammals.
All mammals are warm-blooded. Our bodies have to work to maintain a constant temperature.
Other mammal traits include: breathing air, having hair, giving birth to live young, and providing milk for our young.
The largest heart on this planet is found inside the blue whale; it is the size of a small car!
=
The smallest heart belongs to a tiny frog found in Indonesia.
Ribbit!

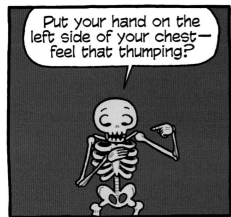

Put your hand on the left side of your chest—feel that thumping?

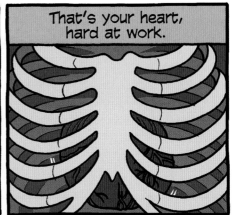

That's your heart, hard at work.

Day in and day out (and at night, too!), it beats, pumping blood throughout your body!

Remember those involuntary actions?

Your heart's beating is one of those magical* involuntary actions...

LUB DUP

...you can't tell it to stop, speed up, or slow down.

LUB DUP

Let's take a look inside the heart!

*not actually magic

67

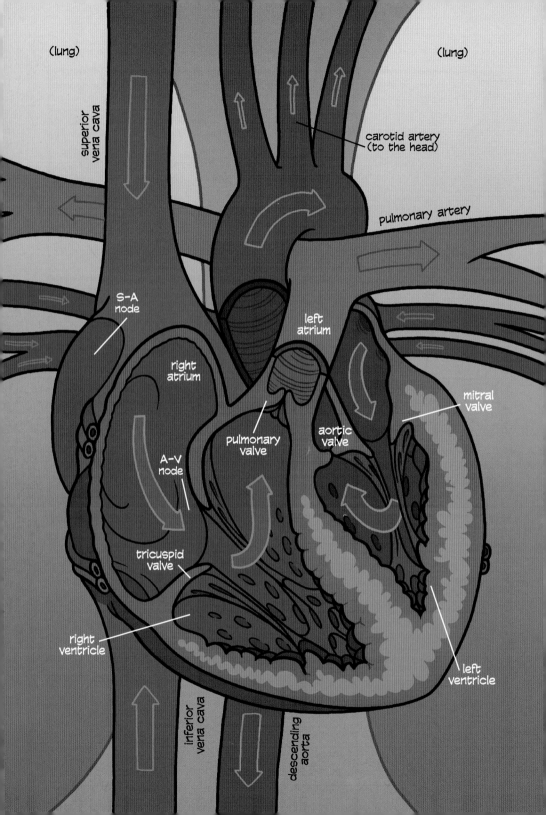

(lung)

(lung)

superior vena cava

carotid artery
(to the head)

pulmonary artery

S-A node

left atrium

right atrium

mitral valve

A-V node

pulmonary valve

aortic valve

tricuspid valve

right ventricle

left ventricle

inferior vena cava

descending aorta

So that's the heart at rest, but let's see it in action.

After all, I am made of muscle.

The heart relaxes, and the valves open, letting both oxygenated and deoxygenated blood into the atria.

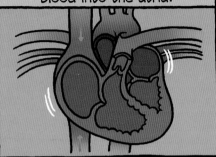

Ventricles fill with blood, and the top atria empty.

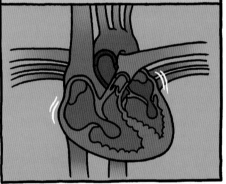

An electrical impulse begins at the S-A node, and the ventricles contract.

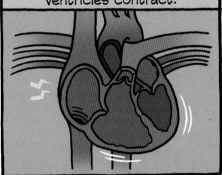

When the ventricles contract, they push blood out of the heart.

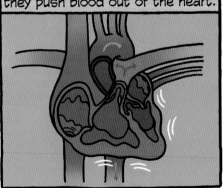

The valves close, and the process begins all over again.

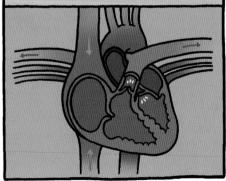

When at rest, the average human heart beats 60-100 times per minute.*

LUB
DUP
LUB
DUP
LUB
DUP

During vigorous exercise, it may beat as many as 170-180 times per minute.

If you want to find your own heart rate, first you must find your pulse.

Place your pointer and middle finger on the palm side of your wrist.

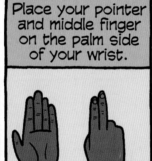

Press gently, and you should feel a dull thumping.

(This is your blood pumping through your arteries, and it corresponds to every heartbeat.)

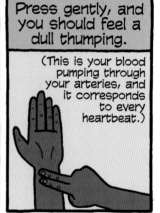

Count the number of thumps that you feel over 15 seconds.

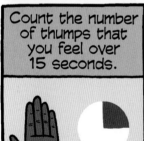

Multiply that number by 4, and you have your heart rate (in beats per minute.)

YOUR NUMBER
×   4
YOUR ♥ RATE

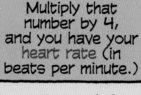

You can even try some exercise and then check your heart rate again to see the difference between your resting and active heart rate.

*Infants and toddlers are actually higher: anywhere from 100-120!

70

Whew! The heart sure has a lot going on!

GLUG GLUG

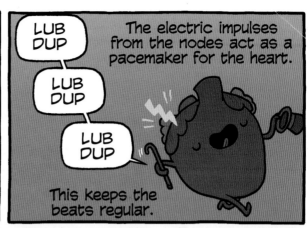

LUB DUP

LUB DUP

LUB DUP

The electric impulses from the nodes act as a pacemaker for the heart.

This keeps the beats regular.

Valves also play a role, not only in the heart, but also in veins.

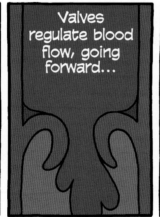

Valves regulate blood flow, going forward...

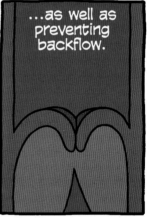

...as well as preventing backflow.

HEART & LUNGS →

In veins, this is especially important—veins carry deoxygenated blood back to the heart and lungs, and it needs to get there quickly and efficiently.

While we're at it, let's take a look at all the routes that carry blood to and from areas of the body.

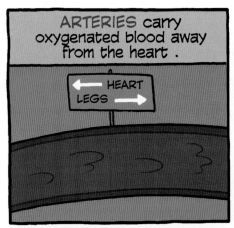

ARTERIES carry oxygenated blood away from the heart.

They branch out into smaller arteries that lead to different areas.

FOOT →
KNEE →
THIGH →

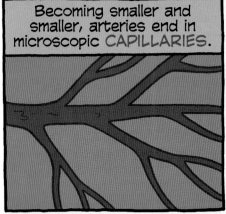

Becoming smaller and smaller, arteries end in microscopic CAPILLARIES.

There, oxygen and nutrients are delivered to the part of the body...in exchange for wastes like carbon dioxide.

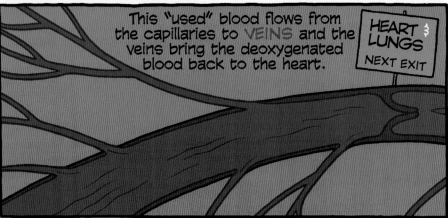

This "used" blood flows from the capillaries to VEINS and the veins bring the deoxygenated blood back to the heart.

HEART & LUNGS
NEXT EXIT

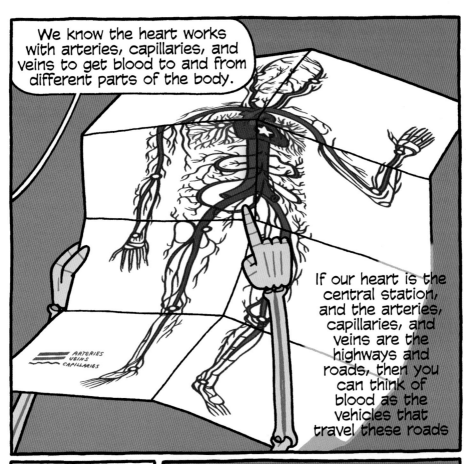

We know the heart works with arteries, capillaries, and veins to get blood to and from different parts of the body.

ARTERIES
VEINS
CAPILLARIES

If our heart is the central station, and the arteries, capillaries, and veins are the highways and roads, then you can think of blood as the vehicles that travel these roads

Ugh, I can never fold these correctly...

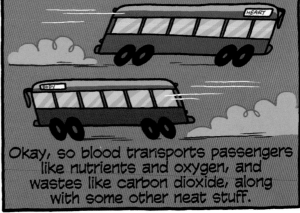

HEART

BODY

Okay, so blood transports passengers like nutrients and oxygen, and wastes like carbon dioxide, along with some other neat stuff.

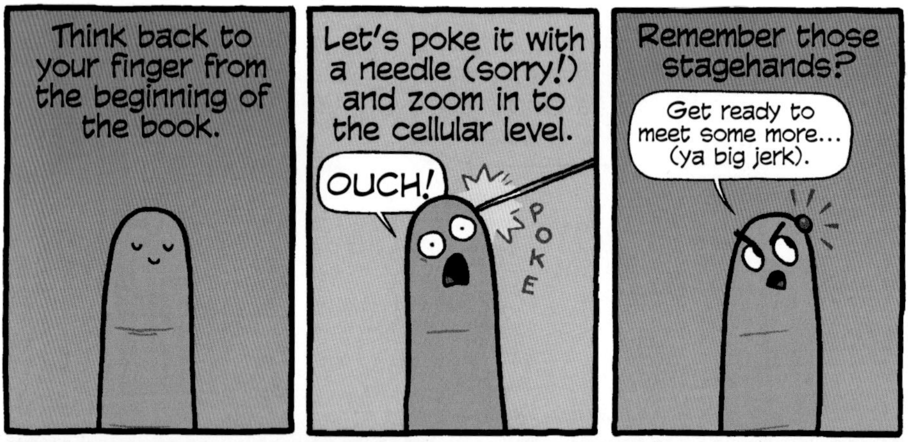
Think back to your finger from the beginning of the book.
Let's poke it with a needle (sorry!) and zoom in to the cellular level.
OUCH!
POKE
Remember those stagehands?
Get ready to meet some more... (ya big jerk).

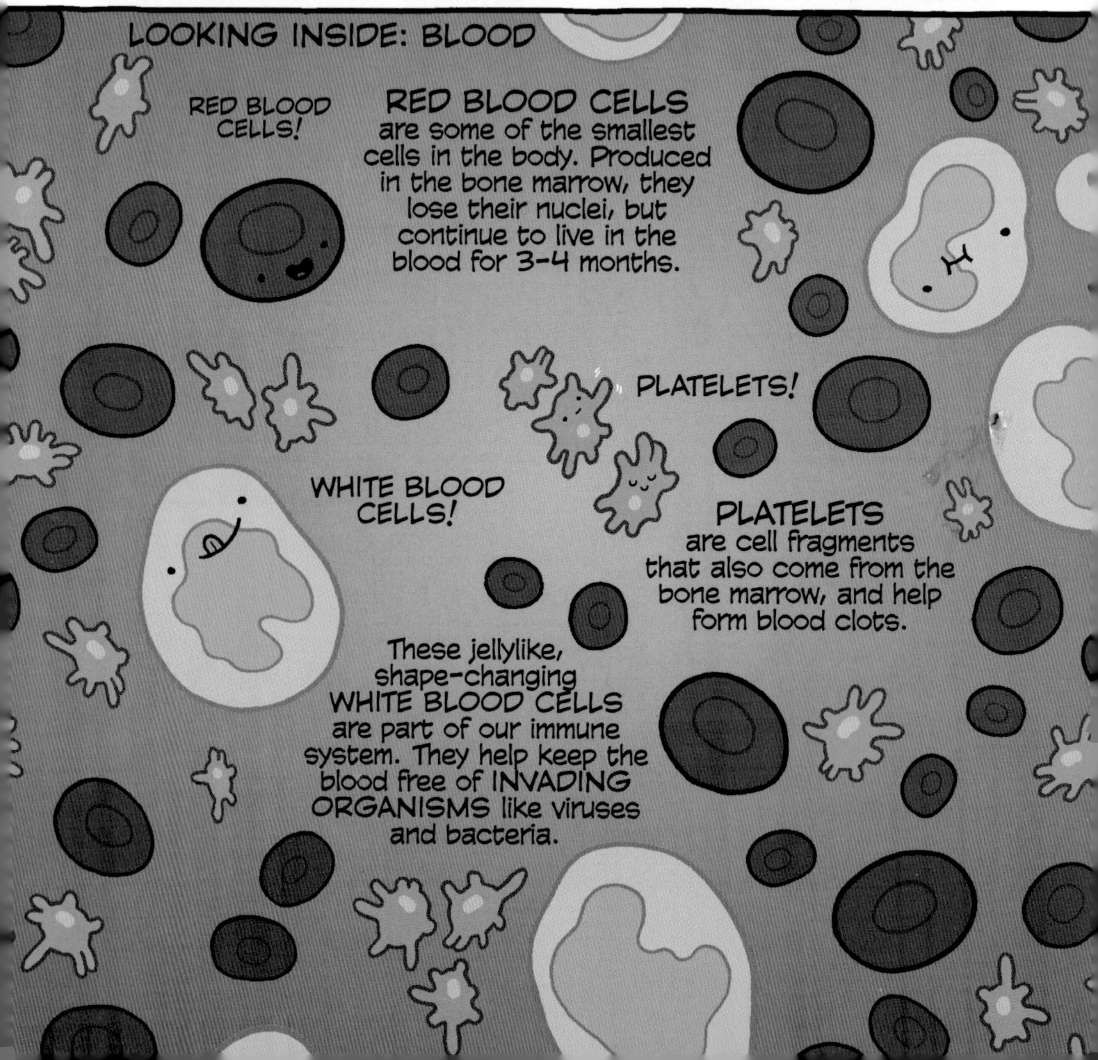
LOOKING INSIDE: BLOOD
RED BLOOD CELLS!
RED BLOOD CELLS are some of the smallest cells in the body. Produced in the bone marrow, they lose their nuclei, but continue to live in the blood for 3-4 months.
PLATELETS!
WHITE BLOOD CELLS!
PLATELETS are cell fragments that also come from the bone marrow, and help form blood clots.
These jellylike, shape-changing WHITE BLOOD CELLS are part of our immune system. They help keep the blood free of INVADING ORGANISMS like viruses and bacteria.

Red blood cells come equipped with a protein called... HEMOGLOBIN!

I use hemoglobin to help me transport OXYGEN, and it makes me bright red!

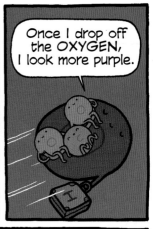

Once I drop off the OXYGEN, I look more purple.

White blood cells keep the blood clean by eating microbes.

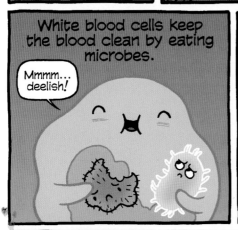

Mmmm... deelish!

I'm so flexible and tiny that I can squeeze in between capillary walls to patrol a larger area—

GOTCHA!!

Blood is 55% plasma.

PLASMA is a pale liquid that is mostly water, with some other nutrients and wastes.

Na Cl
(salts)

P
(proteins)

(sugars)

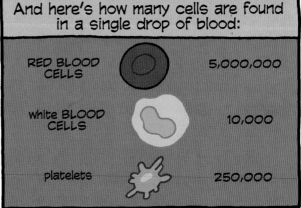

And here's how many cells are found in a single drop of blood:

RED BLOOD CELLS		5,000,000
white BLOOD CELLS		10,000
platelets		250,000

We've seen how blood helps with OXYGEN and NUTRIENT transportation, but what can your blood say about...YOU?

First off, blood helps the body keep a steady TEMPERATURE.

The cardiovascular system CIRCULATES all that warm blood throughout the body.

If you've ever wondered why your fingers, toes, nose, and ears get cold, think about how far away those body parts are from the heart (and how little insulation they have around them.)

The average human body temperature is 98.6 degrees F, but anywhere between 97 and 99.5 degrees F (36.1-37.5 degrees C) is considered normal.

If it's higher than 100.4 degrees F, you have a FEVER, a sign that your body is fighting an infection.

F = Fahrenheit, C = Celsius, both units of measure for temperature

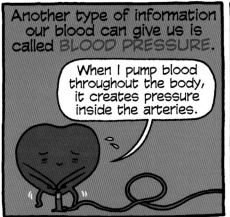

Another type of information our blood can give us is called BLOOD PRESSURE.

When I pump blood throughout the body, it creates pressure inside the arteries.

You can think of it like a bicycle tire—

—when it's inflated, the air inside presses against the walls of the tire, keeping it inflated.

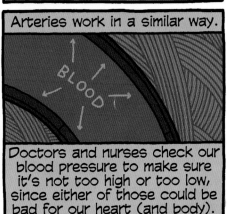

Arteries work in a similar way.

Doctors and nurses check our blood pressure to make sure it's not too high or too low, since either of those could be bad for our heart (and body).

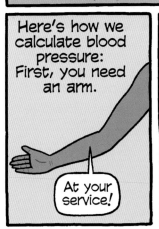

Here's how we calculate blood pressure: First, you need an arm.

At your service!

There is a large artery— the brachial artery—in each arm...

...this is where we will measure your blood pressure.

An inflatable band with a pressure gauge is wrapped around the upper arm.

The band is inflated until it is super tight, squeezing the artery in your arm.

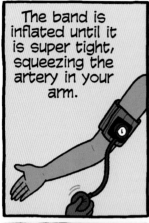

The first reading on the gauge the doctor/nurse looks for is the force your artery can push blood past the squeezed part.

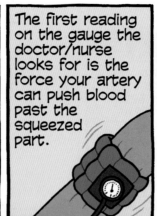

This first number is called your SYSTOLIC PRESSURE.

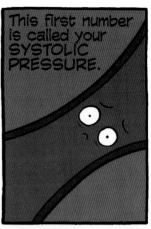

It represents the maximum pressure inside the artery...

...when your heart is beating.

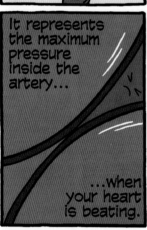

The next number to look for is the minimum pressure...

...when the heart is in between beats.

This number is your DIASTOLIC PRESSURE.

Blood pressure is written like a fraction:

Generally, a healthy range is 100-120 for the top number (systolic pressure) and 60-80 for the bottom number (diastolic pressure).

$$\frac{110}{74}$$

Doctors will also test your blood to make sure you are healthy, or to find out what's wrong if you are sick.

At a glance, all blood looks the same, but there are actually 8 different blood types.

What makes each blood type different is certain proteins (named A, B, or O).

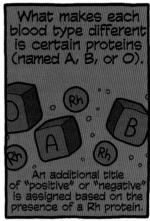

An additional title of "positive" or "negative" is assigned based on the presence of a Rh protein.

Here are all 8 types of blood:

A NEG   A POS   B NEG   B POS   O NEG   O POS   AB NEG   AB POS

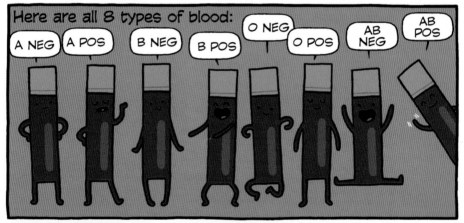

If someone is sick or if they lose a lot of blood (through an injury), they may need a BLOOD TRANSFUSION.

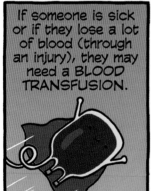

Donated blood is transferred to the sick/injured person's body, but the bloods must be a correct match.*

If not, the wrong blood type can make the person sick.

Me too!

B NEG.

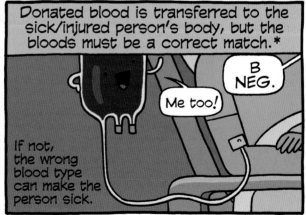

* except for the O blood types; they are compatible with all other types

Speaking of injuries, let's talk about CUTS and SCRAPES.

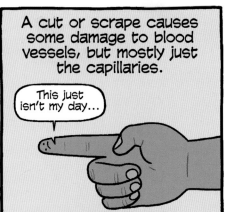

A cut or scrape causes some damage to blood vessels, but mostly just the capillaries.

This just isn't my day...

Once the damage is done, it begins a series of chemical reactions.

Uh, could I get a bandage or something?

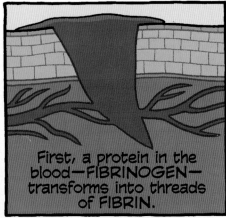

First, a protein in the blood—FIBRINOGEN—transforms into threads of FIBRIN.

These little threads of fibrin crisscross with each other...

FIBRIN

FIBRINO GEN

...forming a meshwork at the site of the damaged blood vessels.

Then platelets stick to the fibrin, and to the walls of the blood vessels.

Pig pile!

Finally, red blood cells join in the fun, sticking to the fibrin and the platelets.

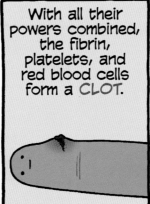

With all their powers combined, the fibrin, platelets, and red blood cells form a CLOT.

But the body isn't done with this cut just yet...

om nom nom

Inside, white blood cells spring to action, seeking out germs (like viruses and bacteria) and eating them.

The clot dries up and hardens—this is called a SCAB.

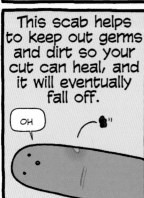

This scab helps to keep out germs and dirt so your cut can heal, and it will eventually fall off.

OH

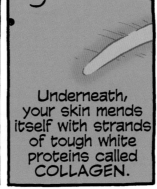

Underneath, your skin mends itself with strands of tough white proteins called COLLAGEN.

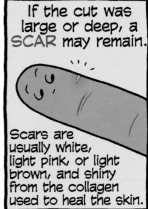

If the cut was large or deep, a SCAR may remain.

Scars are usually white, light pink, or light brown, and shiny from the collagen used to heal the skin.

If a cut is large, deep, or in a sensitive area (like the hands or face), it may need STITCHES to help heal.

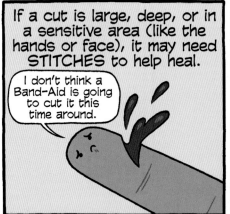

I don't think a Band-Aid is going to cut it this time around.

A cut that reaches a vein will bleed continuously...

It...just won't stop.

...while an artery will spurt.

AAAHH!!!

A cut like this usually involves a trip to the doctor's office or the hospital.

Numbing medicine is either spread or injected around the damaged area.

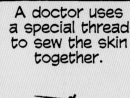

A doctor uses a special thread to sew the skin together.

Stitches will hold the skin in place for a week or two while the body mends itself...

Franken-finger!

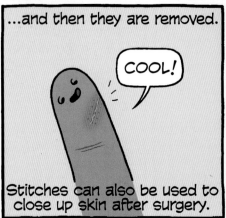

...and then they are removed.

COOL!

Stitches can also be used to close up skin after surgery.

Thanks, finger. You've been a great help.

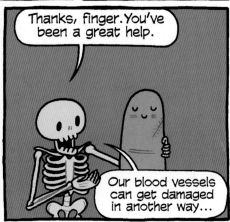

Our blood vessels can get damaged in another way...

BRUISES (also called CONTUSIONS) happen when the soft tissue in the body gets bumped.

yeeeeOW!

BONK

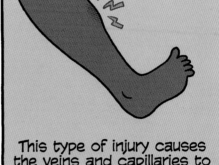

This type of injury causes the veins and capillaries to break under the skin, spilling red blood cells.

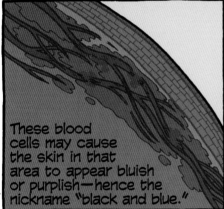

These blood cells may cause the skin in that area to appear bluish or purplish—hence the nickname "black and blue."

At first, the area may be tender and swollen, but it will heal with time.

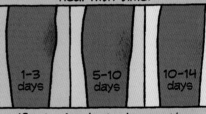

| 1-3 days | 5-10 days | 10-14 days |

If a bruise lasts longer than two weeks, it's a good idea to see a doctor—it may be a sign of a more serious injury.

So that's the cardiovascular system!

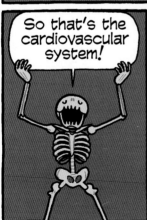

Aside from OXYGEN, there were a whole lot of NUTRIENTS in the blood... where did they all come from?

Surely, you must hunger for knowledge about...

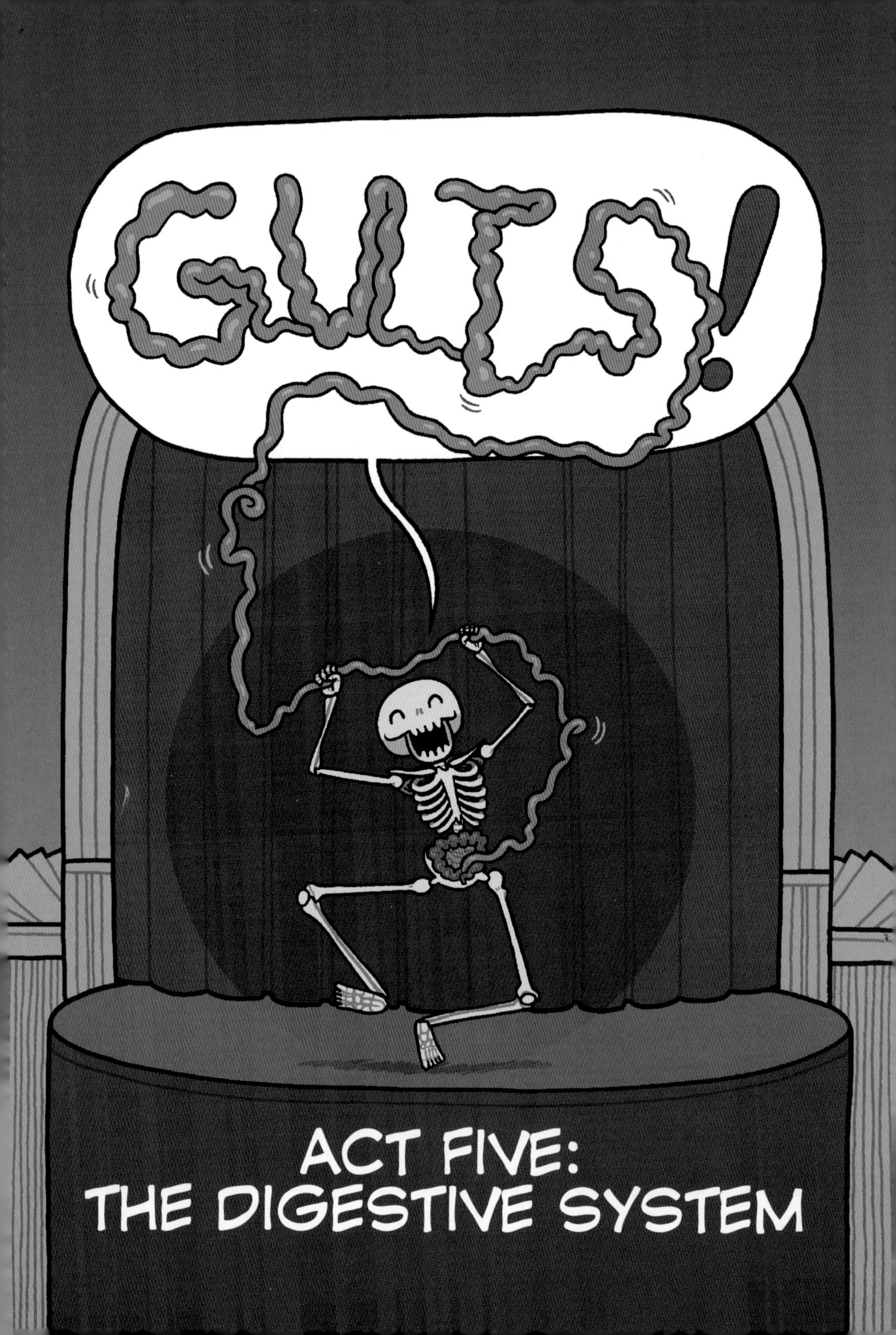
GUTS!
ACT FIVE:
THE DIGESTIVE SYSTEM

Ahem...

Let me just, uh, put these back...

They sure are squishy...

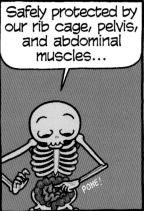
Safely protected by our rib cage, pelvis, and abdominal muscles...

POKE!

...the DIGESTIVE SYSTEM is responsible for breaking down food and turning it into nutrients, which are then used throughout the body.

We've got potential!

I'm full of vitamins and fiber...

...minerals...

...proteins and healthy fats...

...and carbohydrates!

Mmm-hmmmm!

Before we witness food's incredible (but still edible) journey, let's take a look at all the parts that make up the digestive system.

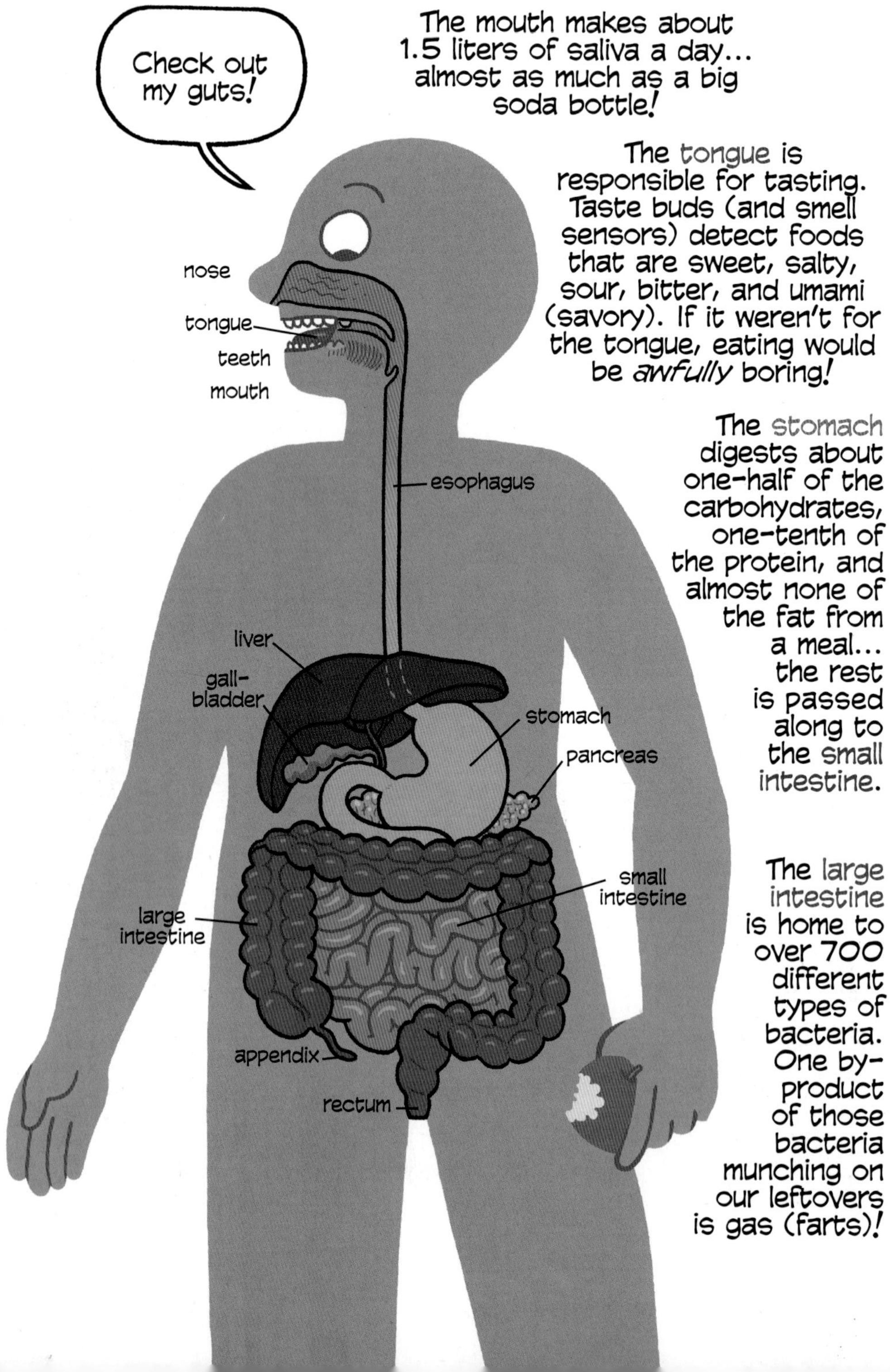

Check out my guts!
The mouth makes about 1.5 liters of saliva a day... almost as much as a big soda bottle!
The tongue is responsible for tasting. Taste buds (and smell sensors) detect foods that are sweet, salty, sour, bitter, and umami (savory). If it weren't for the tongue, eating would be *awfully* boring!
nose
tongue
teeth
mouth
esophagus
The stomach digests about one-half of the carbohydrates, one-tenth of the protein, and almost none of the fat from a meal... the rest is passed along to the small intestine.
liver
gall-bladder
stomach
pancreas
small intestine
large intestine
appendix
rectum
The large intestine is home to over 700 different types of bacteria. One by-product of those bacteria munching on our leftovers is gas (farts)!

The whole system, from mouth to anus, is approximately 30 feet long.

And roughly a half gallon of food and liquid passes through it every day.

30 FT   20 FT   10 FT

Complete digestion can take anywhere from 13 hours to several days, but on average, it takes 18-24 hours.

If you want to time your body's digestion, try this: Eat some corn. Corn is a food that our bodies have a harder time breaking down.

As a result, corn will be present in your feces (poop).

So, from the time that you ingested the corn to the time that it leaves your body... that's how long it took for you to digest it.

BATHROOM

FLUSH

Don't worry— I washed my hands.

BATHROOM

Exactly *WHAT* went on when that corn was inside my body?

Please direct your attention to this peanut butter and banana sandwich!

Greetings, humans.

CARBOHYDRATES

Whole-grain foods, like bread, are considered complex carbohydrates. They are broken down during digestion into GLUCOSE, a sugar that is easily absorbed into the blood.

YEAST

water

flour

FATS and PROTEINS

Protein is found in every cell in the body, and we have to eat things that contain protein to keep our cells fully stocked.

Fats give your body energy and help to absorb vitamins.

SUGARS

Simple carbohydrates are found in fruits, vegetables, and dairy products; they are also broken down into glucose.

banana

peanuts

PEANUT BUTTER

I am made from a few simple ingredients:

But what's really exciting is that I'm going to get eaten.

Here we GOOOOooooo!

88

The mouth is always the scariest part.

CHOMP

YIPES!

Teeth and—

oh, OUCH

—and saliva—

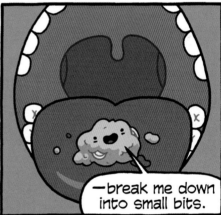

—break me down into small bits.

The tongue allows you to taste food (yum!), but it also shows off its talent as a muscle.

Hi.   Hi.

Thanks to the tongue and teeth, I'm now small enough to be pushed into the...

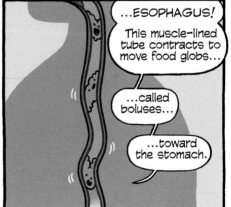

...ESOPHAGUS! This muscle-lined tube contracts to move food globs...

...called boluses...

...toward the stomach.

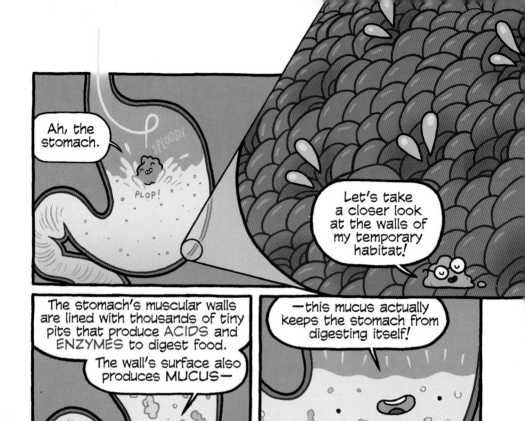

Ah, the stomach.

SPLOOSH

PLOP!

Let's take a closer look at the walls of my temporary habitat!

The stomach's muscular walls are lined with thousands of tiny pits that produce ACIDS and ENZYMES to digest food.

The wall's surface also produces MUCUS—

—this mucus actually keeps the stomach from digesting itself!

The acids and enzymes work to break me down into a soupy liquid called CHYME; being liquid makes nutrients easier to absorb.

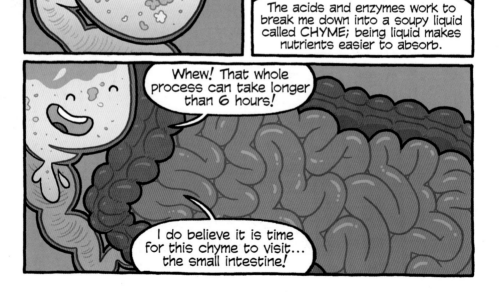

Whew! That whole process can take longer than 6 hours!

I do believe it is time for this chyme to visit... the small intestine!

HEY!!

What about US?!

Oh! Allow me to introduce our digestive system's supporting cast:

Liver!

Gall-bladder!

Pancreas!

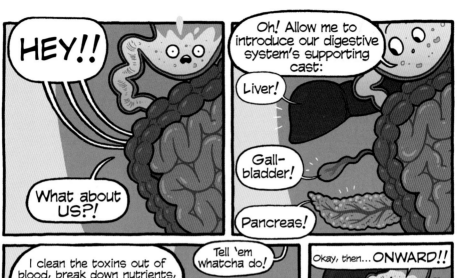

I clean the toxins out of blood, break down nutrients, and store or release sugars, starches, fats, vitamins, and minerals.

Tell 'em whatcha do!

I create salts and bile to help break down fats in the small intestine.

And I create pancreatic juices that also help break down fats. I also play a role in regulating sugar levels in the body.

Okay, then... **ONWARD!!**

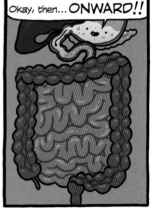

The first section of the small intestine is called the duodenum...

...it connects the stomach to the small intestine.

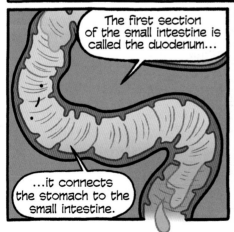

The duodenum breaks down the chyme even more to prepare it for nutrient absorption.

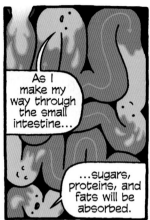

As I make my way through the small intestine...

...sugars, proteins, and fats will be absorbed.

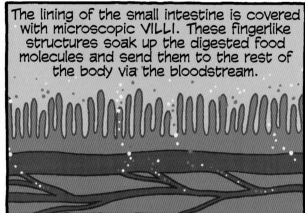

The lining of the small intestine is covered with microscopic VILLI. These fingerlike structures soak up the digested food molecules and send them to the rest of the body via the bloodstream.

The small intestine is about 20 feet long... so this part takes a while.

Goodbye, small intestine...

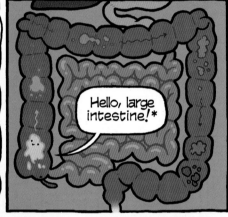

Hello, large intestine!*

By the time I've gotten to the large intestine, most of my nutrients have been absorbed. Now it's time for billions and billions of bacteria to feed on me!

These "good" bacteria are an important part of digestion; they help compact all the leftover wastes.

FOOD!

FOOD!

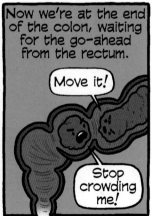

Now we're at the end of the colon, waiting for the go-ahead from the rectum.

Move it!

Stop crowding me!

*Also called the colon.

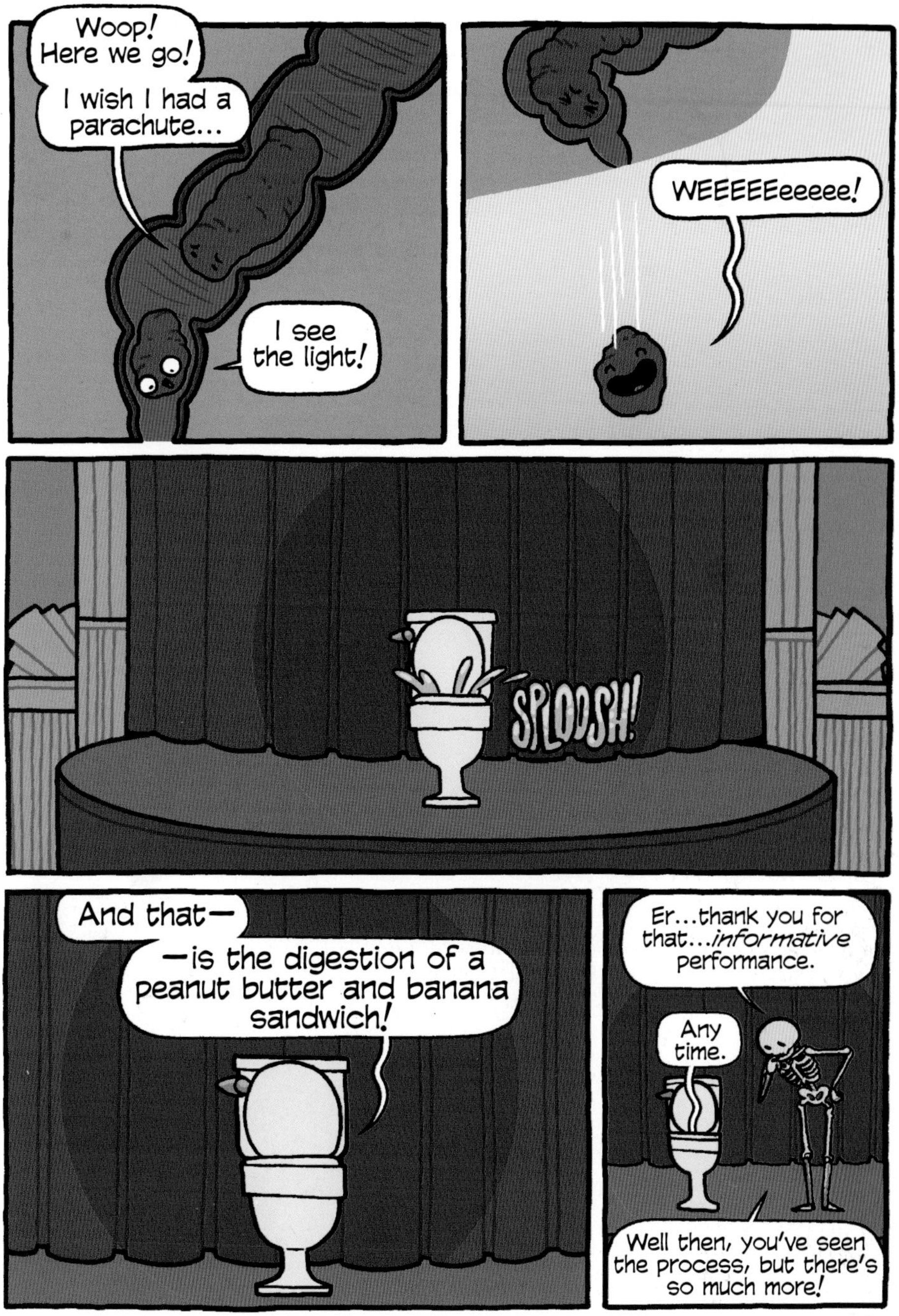
Woop! Here we go!
I wish I had a parachute...
I see the light!
WEEEEEeeeee!
SPLOOSH!
And that—
—is the digestion of a peanut butter and banana sandwich!
Er...thank you for that...*informative* performance.
Any time.
Well then, you've seen the process, but there's so much more!

There was a lot of talk about nutrient absorption, so now we're going to get MOLECULAR.

This is an ENZYME; they are found in our saliva, mucus, tears, stomach juices, etc.

We're EVERYWHERE!!

Enzymes are special proteins that speed up a chemical reaction.

And chemical reactions are what break down foodstuffs into absorbable molecules.

Eyyy... lemme at 'em!

Complex carbohydrates (like bread) are broken down into simple sugars and fiber.

Fiber is indigestible, but that doesn't mean it's bad. It's needed for building feces and moving food through the digestive system.

And simple sugars, also found in fruits and vegetables, are broken down to be used as energy. (Hello again, glucose!)

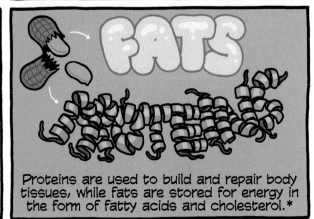

Proteins are used to build and repair body tissues, while fats are stored for energy in the form of fatty acids and cholesterol.*

*similar to enzymes, can you tell?

Foods also contain essential salts, minerals, and vitamins.
Salts!
Minerals!
Vitamins!
Na
Cl
Fe
D
These VITAMINS help your body in many important ways:
I support heathy skin, eyes, immune system, growth and development of cells... and I can be found in milk, eggs, orange and green veggies, and orange fruits.
A
I strengthen bones by helping the body absorb calcium, and I can be found in sunlight, egg yolks, fish oil, and fortified milk.
D
I help form collagen and help wounds heal, as well as supporting healthy bones, teeth, gums, blood vessels, and brains.
I can be found in red berries, red and green peppers, tomatoes, broccoli, spinach, grapefruit, and oranges.
C
I protect cells from damage and I'm great for red blood cells.
I can be found in vegetable oils, nuts, green leafy vegetables, avocados, and whole grains.
E
I help make red blood cells and keep brain cells healthy.
I can be found in fish, red meat, poultry, milk, cheese, and eggs.
B 12
I support brain function and break down proteins, helping to make red blood cells.
I can be found in potatoes, bananas, beans, seeds, nuts, red meat, poultry, fish, eggs, and spinach.
B 6
I convert carbohydrates into energy, and support muscle and brain health.
I can be found in fortified bread, cereals, and pasta, as well as meat, fish, beans, peas, and soy.
B 1
I help convert food into energy, and keep your skin and brain cells healthy.
I can be found in red meat, poultry, fish, and peanuts.
B 3
I also help convert carbohydrates into energy and make red blood cells.
I can be found in fortified breads and cereals, milk, leafy vegetables, mushrooms, and almonds.
z
B 2
I help with cell growth and make red blood cells!
I can be found in dark leafy greens, Brussels sprouts, root vegetables, avocados, milk, and fortified breads and cereals.
B 9

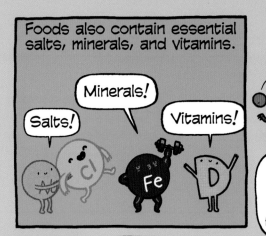

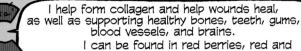

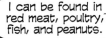

And let's not forget about MINERALS.
These are specific ELEMENTS that are good for our body:

I build and maintain healthy bones and teeth, and I can be found in dairy products, broccoli, dark leafy greens, and calcium-fortified foods.

CALCIUM!

I help red blood cells carry oxygen throughout the body, and I can be found in red meat, pork, fish, shellfish, poultry, lentils, beans, soy, dark leafy greens, and raisins.

IRON!

I keep your muscles, brain, heart, and bones healthy. I also produce proteins and create energy from food. You can find me in whole grains, nuts, seeds, dark leafy greens, potatoes, bananas, and dark chocolate.

MAGNESIUM!

I support healthy bones and teeth, and also help convert energy from food. I can be found in dairy products, meat, and fish.

PHOSPHOROUS!

I help your muscles and your brain, and support the kidneys. You can find me in broccoli, potato skins, dark leafy greens, citrus fruits, bananas, dried fruits, legumes, peas, and beans.

POTASSIUM!

I support cell growth and your immune system, as well as help heal wounds. I can be found in red meat, poultry, oysters, nuts, beans, soy, dairy products, and whole grains.

ZINC!

Maybe the most important thing that you put in your body is WATER.

That's right.

Without water, our bodies wouldn't work. Water is in our blood, cells, skin, digestive juices... almost everything!

All these nutrients help the body to function properly, but there are some—

BUUUUUURP!

My goodness! Excuse me!

As I was saying, there are some rather *interesting* things that happen to the digestive system.

Burping, for instance. When we eat or drink, we also swallow air.

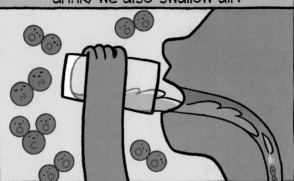

That air contains gases like oxygen, nitrogen, and carbon dioxide.

These extra gases are forced from the stomach, up the esophagus and finally out of the mouth, in the form of a—

BURP!

Soda contains carbon dioxide. (Those are the bubbles!)

It is this gas that creates an even BIGGER burp.

Burping is totally natural, just remember to say "excuse me" or close your mouth when you release those stomach gases.

Not all the air that we swallow makes it out as a burp. Some of it travels ALL the way through the digestive system.

POOT

Pardon me!

These gases, added to the gases produced by the large intestine as it breaks down food, go on to become what we affectionately call farts.*

Good bacteria in the large intestine produce AMMONIA and HYDROGEN SULFIDE, which...

...along with HYDROGEN, CARBON DIOXIDE, and METHANE, give farts their rather pungent odor.

Some foods can make you more gassy than others.

We're a bit of a challenge for your intestines.

Intestinal gas can also be caused by certain foods— a LACTOSE INTOLERANT person may get more gas and cramping due to lactose (a sugar) found in dairy products.

Sorry 'bout that!

Everyone farts, but just like with burping, it's important to be polite.

*aka flatus, intestinal gas, toots, whizz pops, barking spiders, etc....

Sometimes things don't always go so smoothly in the digestive system.

You've probably had a stomachache or diarrhea or vomiting at some point in your life.

These things can happen to anybody.

GURGLE!!

When your digestive system isn't working correctly, it can be very uncomfortable, but it's your body's natural way of dealing with a number of problems.

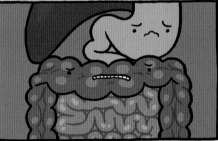

Let's look at the whats, hows, and whys of some digestive ailments:

STOMACHACHE

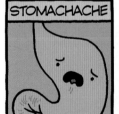

Often called indigestion or dyspepsia, a stomachache is perhaps the most common digestive system problem.

Stomachaches can be caused by many things:

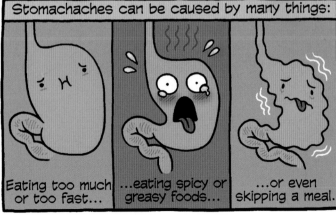

Eating too much or too fast...

...eating spicy or greasy foods...

...or even skipping a meal.

HEARTBURN

Heartburn, despite its name, has nothing to do with the heart.

Characterized by a burning sensation in the chest, heartburn is caused by stomach acids coming up and irritating the esophagus.

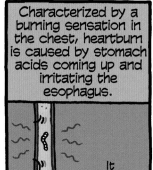

It buurns.

What makes the stomach acids do this? The same culprits that cause stomachaches!

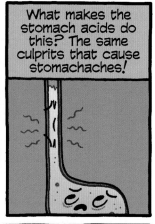

Vomit is a mixture of half-digested food and stomach juices (acids) that leave the body through the mouth.

Vomiting can be caused by a number of things: an infection of the stomach or small intestine (often called a "stomach bug"), motion sickness, or even nervousness.

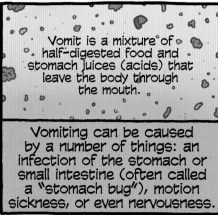

For whatever the reason, your digestive system says—

"FREEZE!"

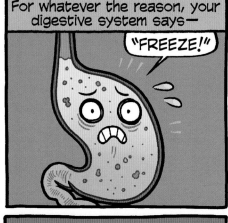

—and stops everything, contracting the muscles in the stomach and small intestine to push digested food up through the esophagus and out of the mouth.

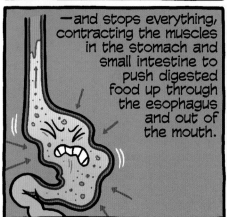

Yeah, you can pretty much picture what that would look like...

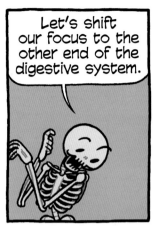

Let's shift our focus to the other end of the digestive system.

First up: DIARRHEA...

Diarrhea is characterized by runny, watery bowel movements.

And let me tell you what you already know: it is NOT pleasant.

Diarrhea can be caused by illnesses like the stomach bug, contamined food, or stress.

GURGLE
GURGLE

When you have diarrhea, your body loses A LOT of water, making it easy to become dehydrated...so be sure to drink plenty of water.

Another lower digestive system situation is...

CONSTIPATION

Um, we've got a traffic jam down here...

If you haven't pooped in a while, if it hurts to go to the bathroom, or if your bowel movements are hard, you might be constipated.

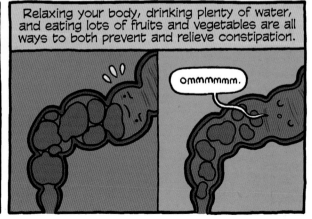

Relaxing your body, drinking plenty of water, and eating lots of fruits and vegetables are all ways to both prevent and relieve constipation.

ommmmmm.

Now, let's take a closer look at some of the troublemakers causing digestive distress.

GASTROENTERITIS!

YAH!

The "stomach bug," the "stomach virus," and the "stomach flu" are all names for GASTROENTERITIS.

Sounds fancy, doesn't it?

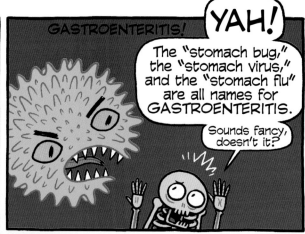

Usually caused by a virus, its symptoms include stomach cramps, nausea, vomiting, diarrhea, and fever.

HEH HEH

I'm a big [little] jerk!

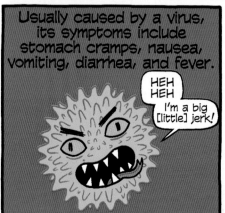

Gastroenteritis is contagious—it can be spread from person to person. If you are sick, be sure to wash your hands and do not share food or drinks.

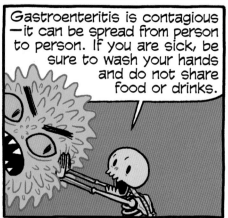

FOOD POISONING is another form of digestive dilemma. It does not mean that your food was poisoned.

But it does mean that your food contained a bacteria (or virus).

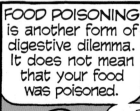

Food poisoning can cause vomiting or diarrhea (or both!).

Yeah, we're jerks, too!

Foods from animals (like meat and eggs), raw foods, and unwashed fruits and vegetables can carry germs that cause food poisoning.

Always wash your hands before eating, thoroughly wash fruits and veggies, and cook food (like meats) to the correct temperature.

There are a few other types of tummy trauma—remember that little dangle-y thing hanging off the large intestine?

The appendix.

For a long time, scientists thought that I had no function.

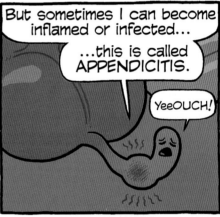

Now they believe that I play an important role in the immune system's development when humans are young. And that I act as a special storage area for healthy gut bacteria.

But sometimes I can become inflamed or infected...

...this is called APPENDICITIS.

YeeOUCH!

An inflamed appendix will usually cause pain in the lower right side of the abdomen, and it can be serious (but fixable).

Doctors can actually remove an inflamed appendix...

...but I don't think they let you keep it.

Looks like this is goodbye...

Stomachaches, vomiting, constipation, and diarrhea can also be caused by...

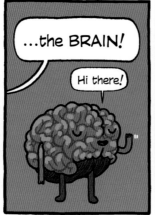

...the BRAIN!

Hi there!

It may come as a surprise...

Um, what are you doing?

...but stress and anxiety can affect your digestive system (and other parts of your body).

Put me down!

I HATE heights!

Whether we are aware of it or not, how we think and feel can have physical effects.

I— I don't f-feel so well...

Ugh... me neither.

Okay, brain, listen up—we need to calm down. Let's take a few deep breaths...

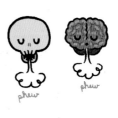

phew   phew

...and try to relax.

Relaxing and removing stress isn't just healthy for your mind; it's good for your whole body.

Here are some other ways to keep your digestive system in good working order:

DRINK WATER!

If you haven't figured it out already, water is super-good for you.

After all, our bodies are roughly 60% water.

EAT FOODS RICH IN FIBER!

Fruits and vegetables will help keep your bowel movements regular.

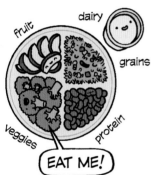

fruit

dairy

grains

veggies

protein

EAT ME!

A well-balanced diet will also help keep you and your body healthy.

DON'T OVEREAT or EAT TOO FAST!

Both of these things can cause stomachaches.

Also, avoid eating right before bed; our body digests best when we are awake and active.

GET PLENTY OF REST AND SLEEP!

z z z Z

The body needs regular sleep to stay healthy, so catch those zzz's.

You probably do all those things already; it's just nice to be reminded of how they help our body stay healthy.

We've spent so much time talking about foods...

...now it's time to turn our attention to how the body manages LIQUIDS...

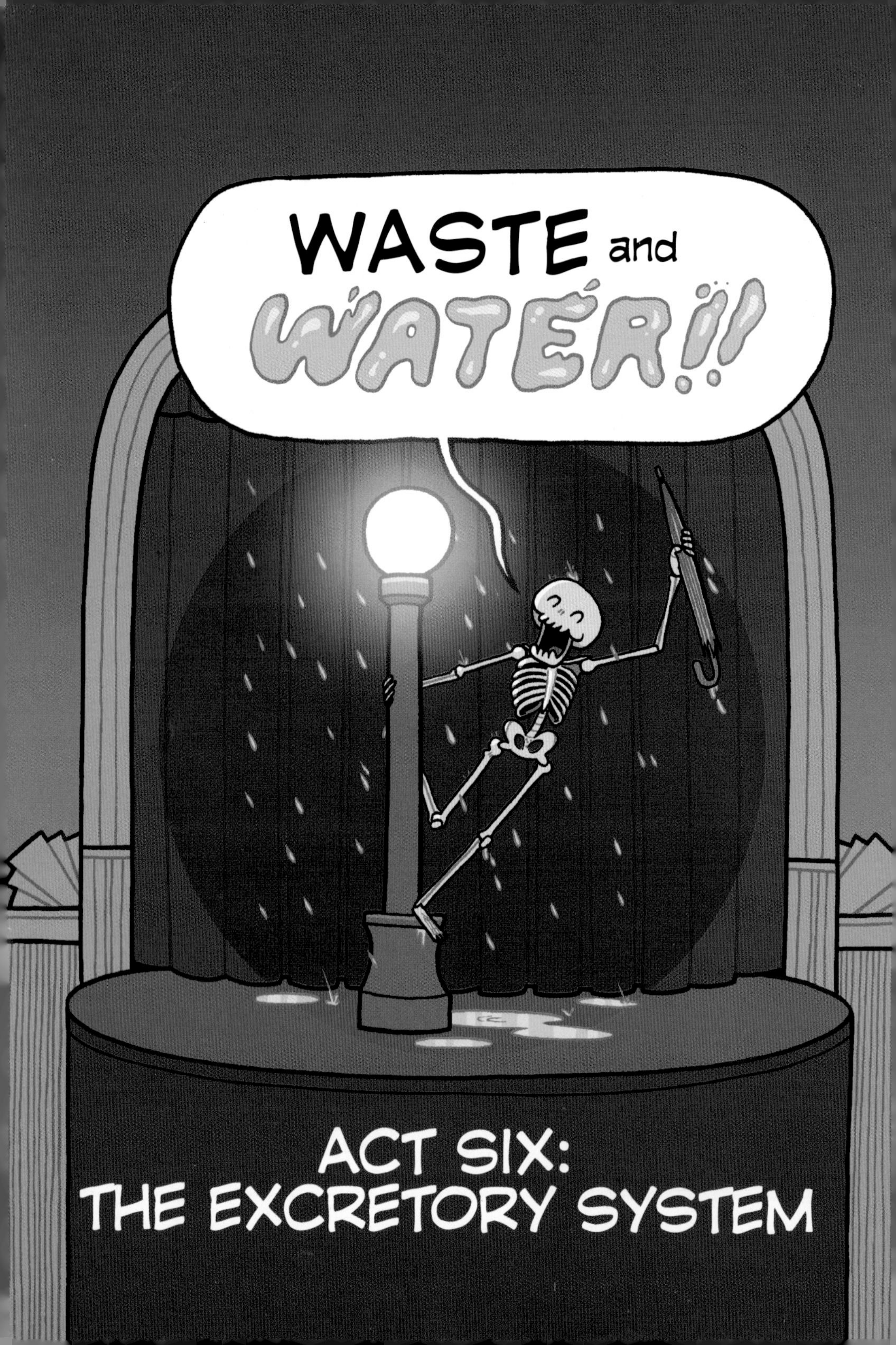
WASTE and WATER!!
ACT SIX:
THE EXCRETORY SYSTEM

I've said it before and I'll say it again: WATER is pretty darn important—

FLIP
FLIP FLIP

—to our health, our bodies, even our planet!

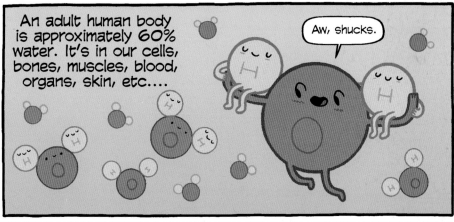

An adult human body is approximately 60% water. It's in our cells, bones, muscles, blood, organs, skin, etc....

Aw, shucks.

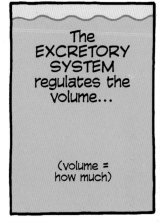

The EXCRETORY SYSTEM regulates the volume...

(volume = how much)

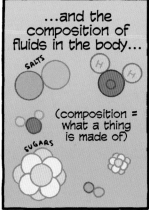

...and the composition of fluids in the body...

SALTS

(composition = what a thing is made of)

SUGARS

...as well as removing liquid wastes and extra fluid.

Let's take a look at the body parts that make this water management possible:

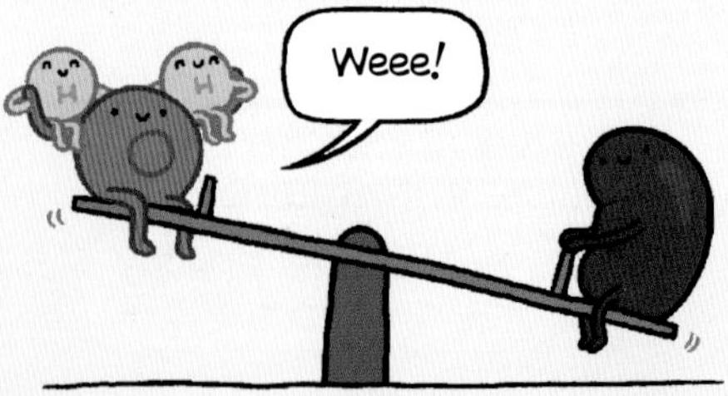
Weee!

The excretory system is resposible for water balance: the kidneys filter water and extract wastes, which are released from the body in the form of urine.

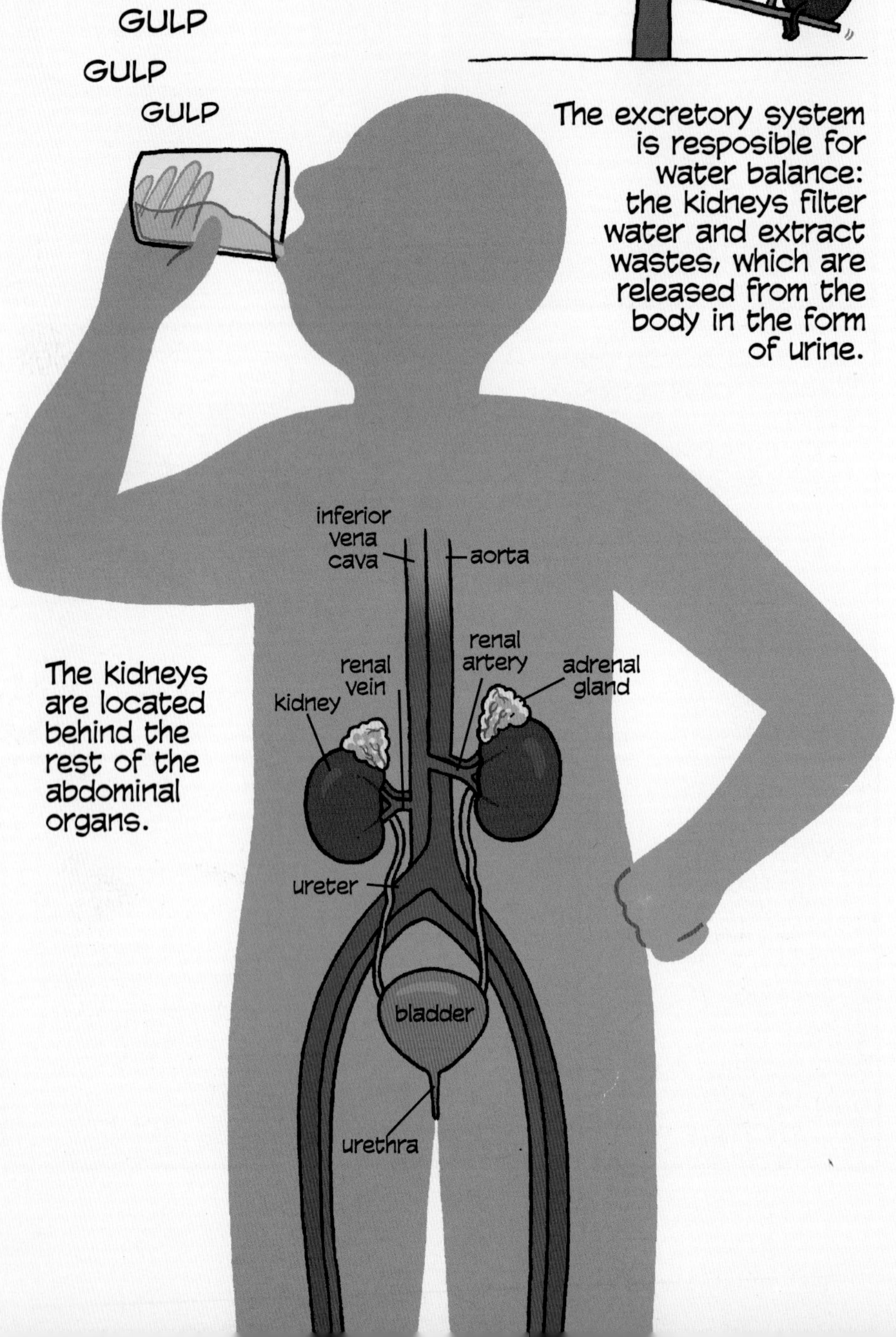
GULP
GULP
GULP
inferior vena cava
aorta
renal vein
renal artery
adrenal gland
kidney
ureter
bladder
urethra

The kidneys are located behind the rest of the abdominal organs.

It's recommended that human beings should drink about 8 glasses (.5 gallons or 2 liters) of water every day to maintain fluids in the body...

...but really it depends on lots of things: your age, your height and weight, whether or not you've been exercising, even the temperature outside!

Instead of counting glasses, remember to drink water when you're thristy, at every meal, and before, during, and after exercise!

Water is lost when we urinate, sweat, and exhale.

OOF!

That last one—exhaling—might seem a bit weird, but think of your breath on a cold day.

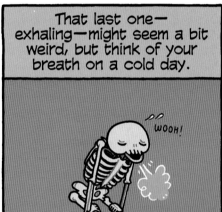

WOOH!

That "steam" you see when you breathe out?

That's WATER VAPOR!

PPHHHEW!

Let's take a look at what's going on inside the excretory system...

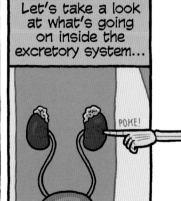

POKE!

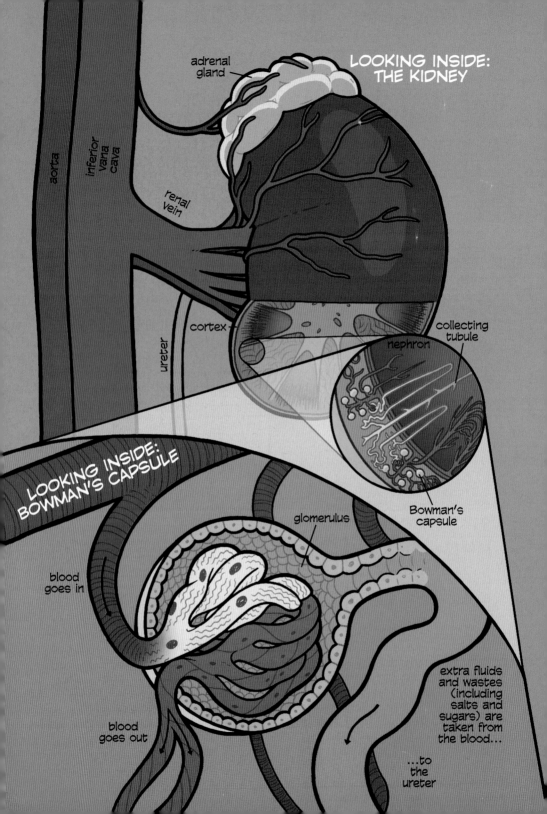

adrenal
gland

aorta

inferior
vana
cava

renal
vein

ureter

cortex

nephron

collecting
tubule

Bowman's
capsule

LOOKING INSIDE:
BOWMAN'S CAPSULE

glomerulus

blood
goes in

blood
goes out

extra fluids
and wastes
(including
salts and
sugars) are
taken from
the blood...

...to
the
ureter

The kidneys filter about 440 gallons (2,000 liters) of blood each day...

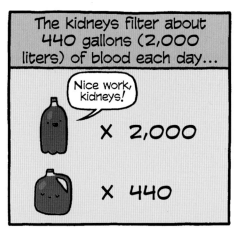

Nice work, kidneys!

X 2,000

X 440

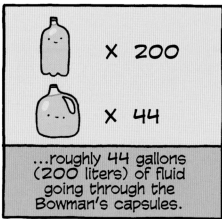

X 200

X 44

...roughly 44 gallons (200 liters) of fluid going through the Bowman's capsules.

Almost all this liquid is put back into the blood...

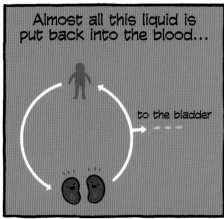

to the bladder

See ya later.

...with only .2-.4 gallons (1-2 liters) of liquid leaving the body as urine every day.

While we're on the topic of urine, let's follow this liquid down the ureters and into...

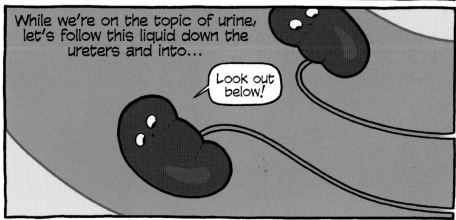

Look out below!

...the bladder! This muscular organ is a temporary home for all that extra liquid expelled from the kidneys.

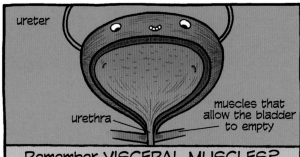

ureter

urethra

muscles that allow the bladder to empty

Remember VISCERAL MUSCLES? These specialized muscles form the walls of our internal organs, and the bladder is one of them.

LOOKING INSIDE: THE BLADDER

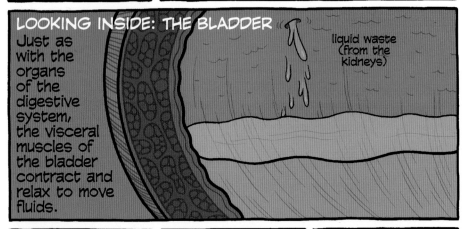

Just as with the organs of the digestive system, the visceral muscles of the bladder contract and relax to move fluids.

liquid waste (from the kidneys)

The bladder can hold approximately .07 gallons (.3 liters) of urine.

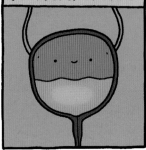

As it fills, the need to expel its urine is felt along the urethra.

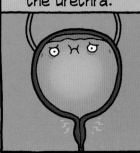

This signals to the brain that it's time to urinate (pee!).

Phew!

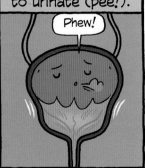

Us humans urinate an average of 3-4 times a day.

The color of your urine can actually tell you something about your body: clear, pale yellow urine signifies a well-hydrated body...

...while dark yellow or cloudy urine is a sign that you should drink more water.

Well, that's an easy problem to fix.

Eating a bunch of beets can make your urine pink! That's because of the beets' color...

...they can sometimes make your poop purple!

All this talk of liquids and releasing wastes...

...I think I need to use the restroom!

This would be a good time for—

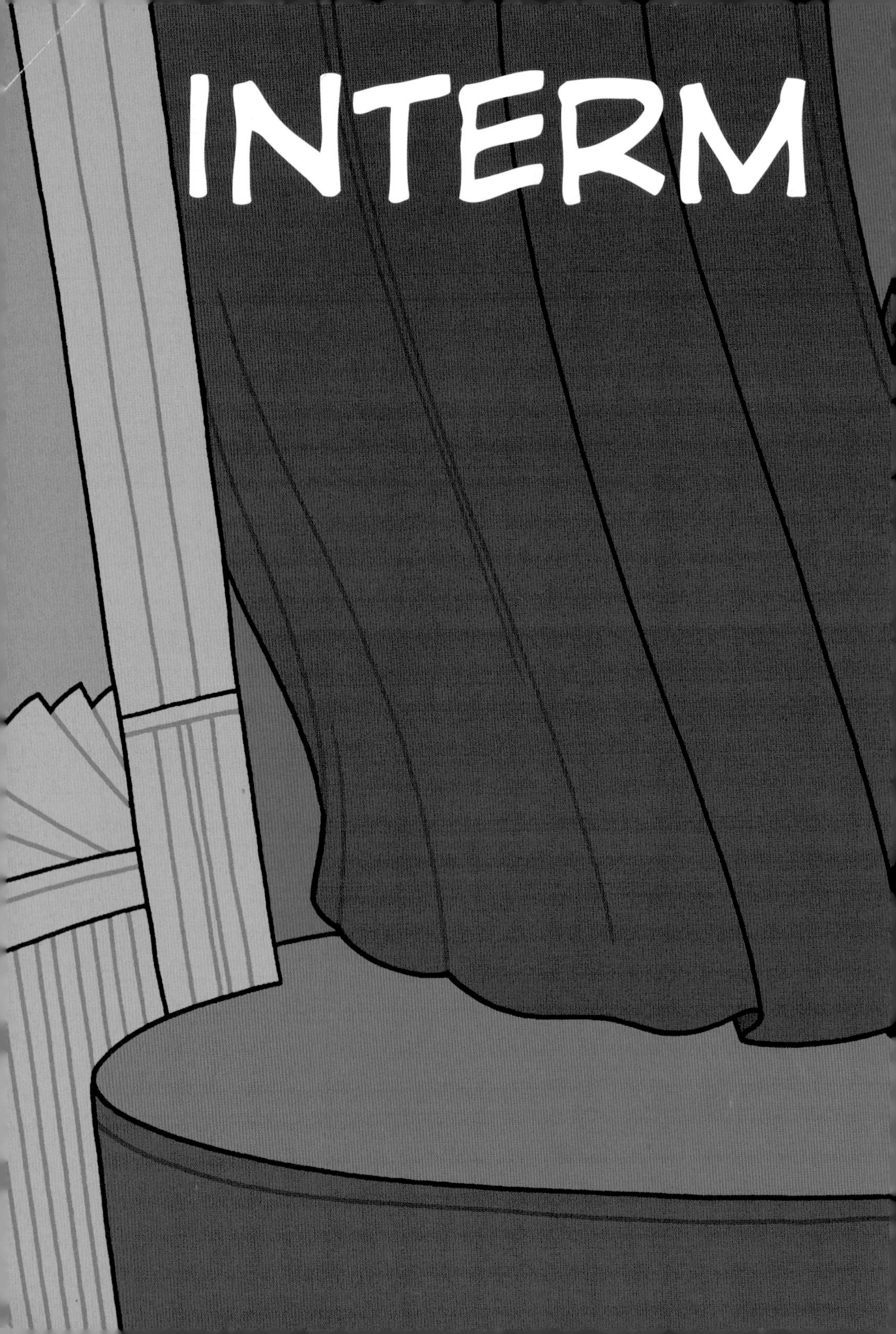
INTERM

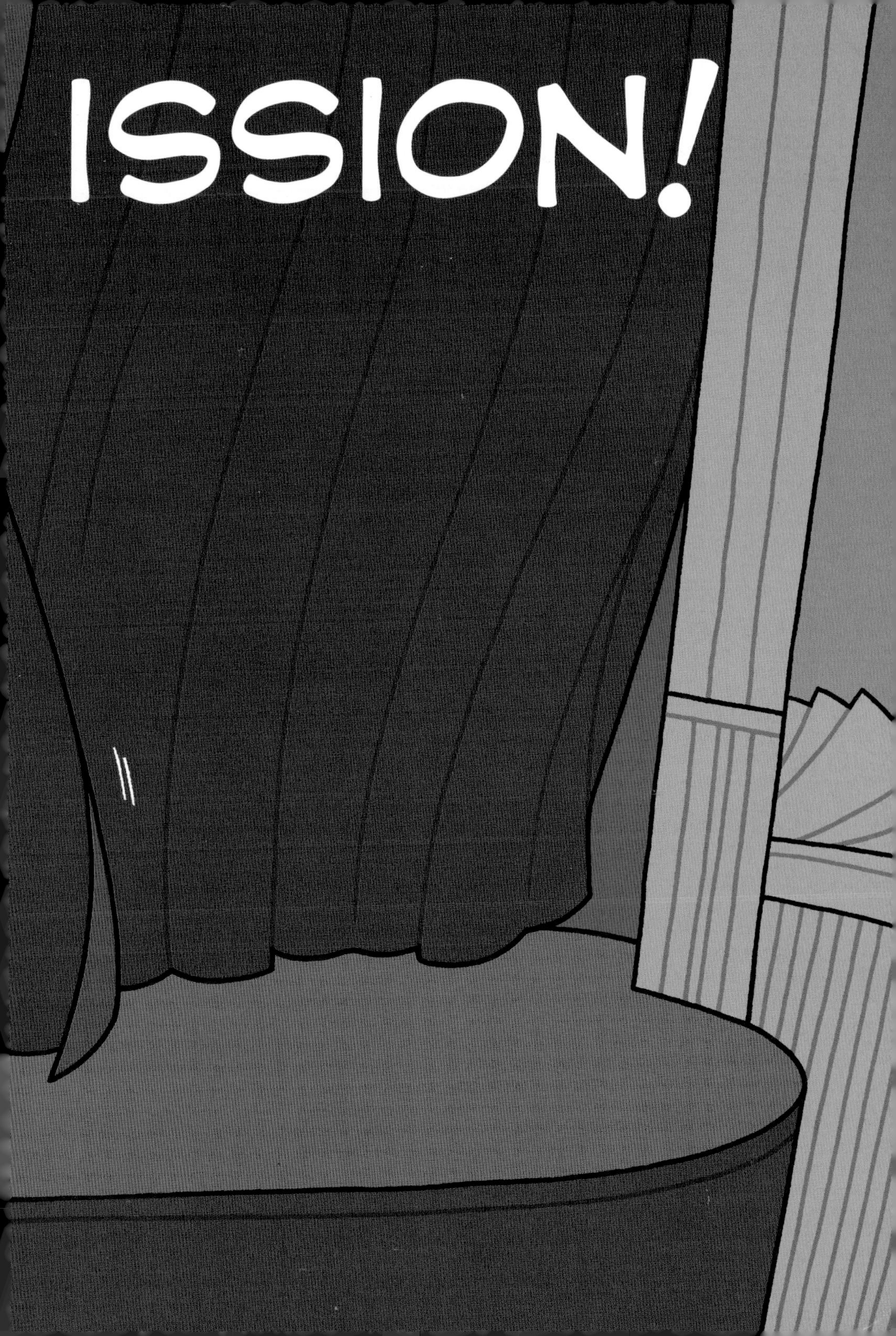
ISSION!

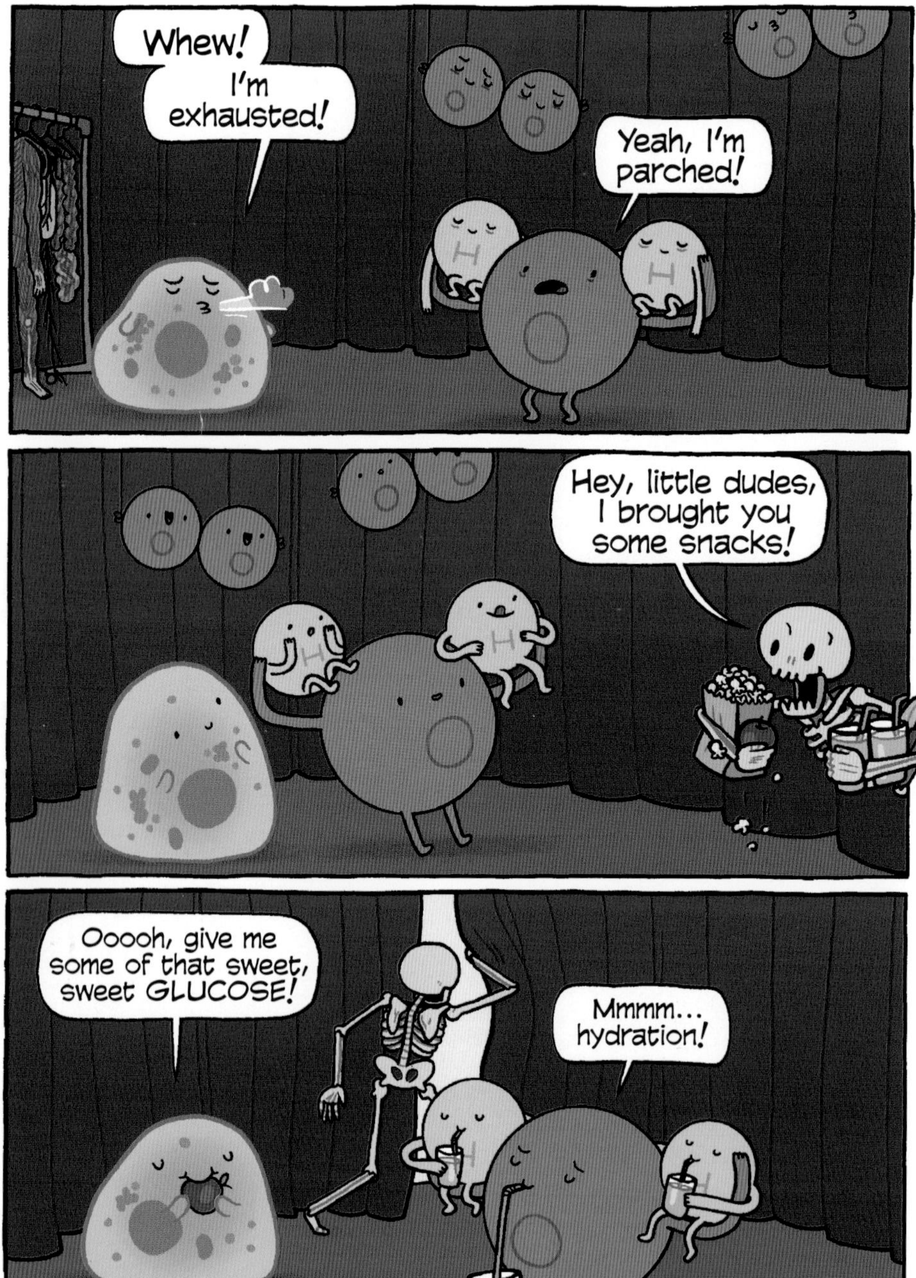
Whew!
I'm exhausted!
Yeah, I'm parched!
Hey, little dudes, I brought you some snacks!
Ooooh, give me some of that sweet, sweet GLUCOSE!
Mmmm... hydration!

Ah, much better.

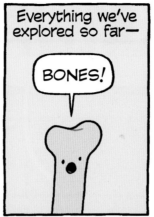

Everything we've explored so far—

BONES!

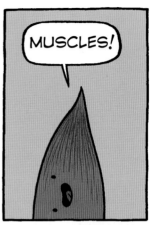

MUSCLES!

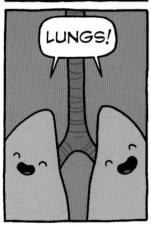

LUNGS!

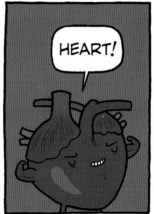

HEART!

GUTS!

—how do they all know what to do?

I mean, I know that my brain signals my legs to walk or my mouth to talk...

...but I don't need to tell my bones to grow, or my stomach to digest. That's a job for...

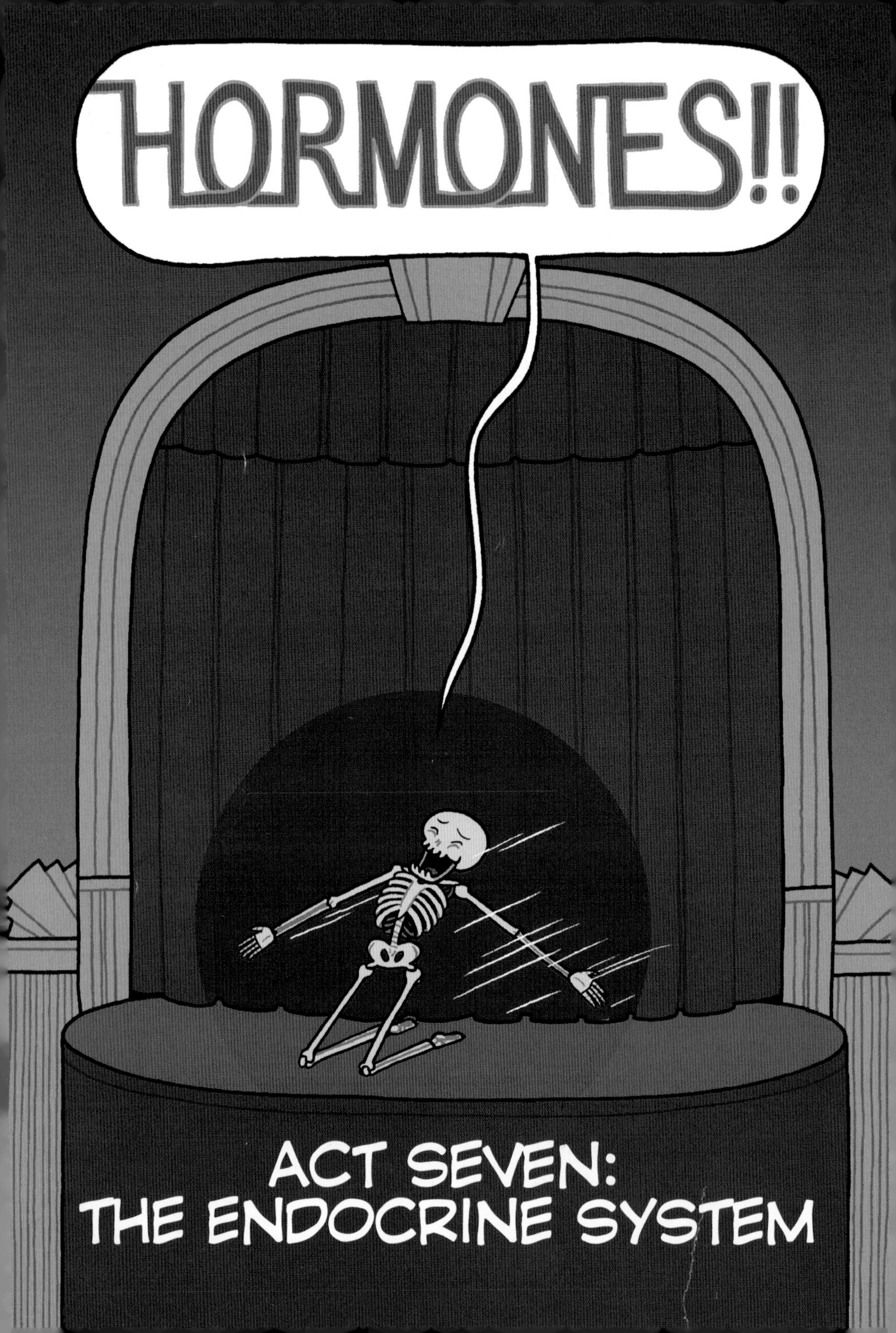
HORMONES!!
ACT SEVEN:
THE ENDOCRINE SYSTEM

This may be the ENDOCRINE SYSTEM but it sure ain't the END-O-THIS show!

HA HA HAHA HA HA HAH

ha...ha...I crack myself up...but seriously...

The ENDOCRINE SYSTEM is a network of GLANDS that produce HORMONES.

HORMONES are the body's chemical messengers—they broadcast directions to the other systems, telling them what to do.

Hormones regulate metabolism, water-salt balance, growth, sexual development, and even reaction to stress.

Delivery for the stomach!

Thanks!

THE ENODCRINE SYSTEM

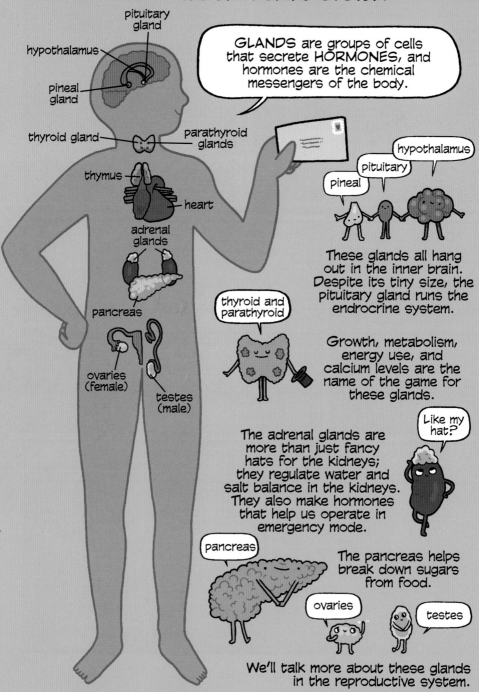

pituitary gland

hypothalamus

pineal gland

thyroid gland

parathyroid glands

thymus

heart

adrenal glands

pancreas

ovaries (female)

testes (male)

GLANDS are groups of cells that secrete HORMONES, and hormones are the chemical messengers of the body.

hypothalamus

pituitary

pineal

These glands all hang out in the inner brain. Despite its tiny size, the pituitary gland runs the endrocrine system.

thyroid and parathyroid

Growth, metabolism, energy use, and calcium levels are the name of the game for these glands.

Like my hat?

The adrenal glands are more than just fancy hats for the kidneys; they regulate water and salt balance in the kidneys. They also make hormones that help us operate in emergency mode.

pancreas

The pancreas helps break down sugars from food.

ovaries

testes

We'll talk more about these glands in the reproductive system.

So, the brain is like mission control, with the hypothalamus watching over all the glands...

POKE

...and the glands are regulating all sorts of bodily functions and actions...

...and their instructions are carried around by hormones.

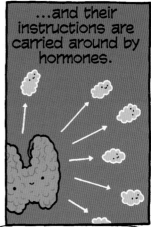

The human body produces over 50 different hormones, and each of these hormones has a different job. Here are just a few of the hormones that keep our body working.

I help with your sleep cycle.

MELATONIN

I make you feel happy when you accomplish a task.

DOPAMINE

I regulate heart rate, blood vessel and airway constriction/expansion, and metabolism!

ADRENALINE

I help cells to absorb glucose from the blood.

INSULIN

HUMAN GROWTH HORMONE

I do just that—stimulate growth, as well as cell reproduction and regeneration.

And I stimulate the release of stomach acids.

GASTRIN

Hormones travel all over the body via the bloodstream, delivering instructions.

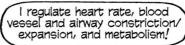

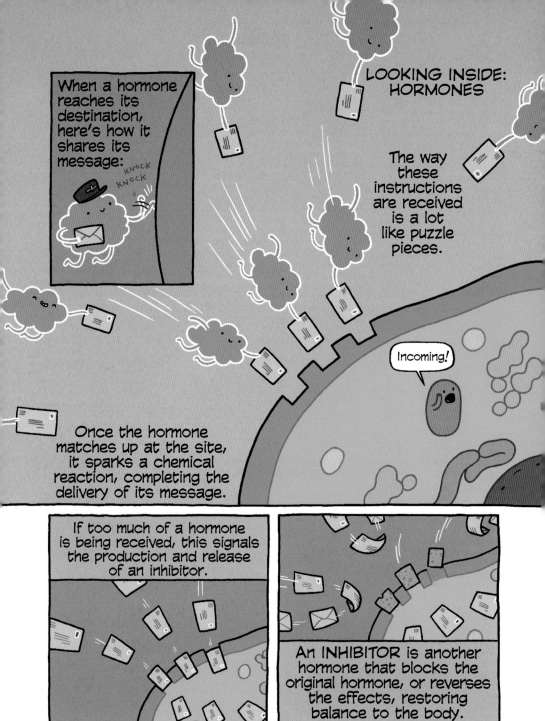

When a hormone reaches its destination, here's how it shares its message:

KNOCK KNOCK

LOOKING INSIDE: HORMONES

The way these instructions are received is a lot like puzzle pieces.

Incoming!

Once the hormone matches up at the site, it sparks a chemical reaction, completing the delivery of its message.

If too much of a hormone is being received, this signals the production and release of an inhibitor.

An INHIBITOR is another hormone that blocks the original hormone, or reverses the effects, restoring balance to the body.

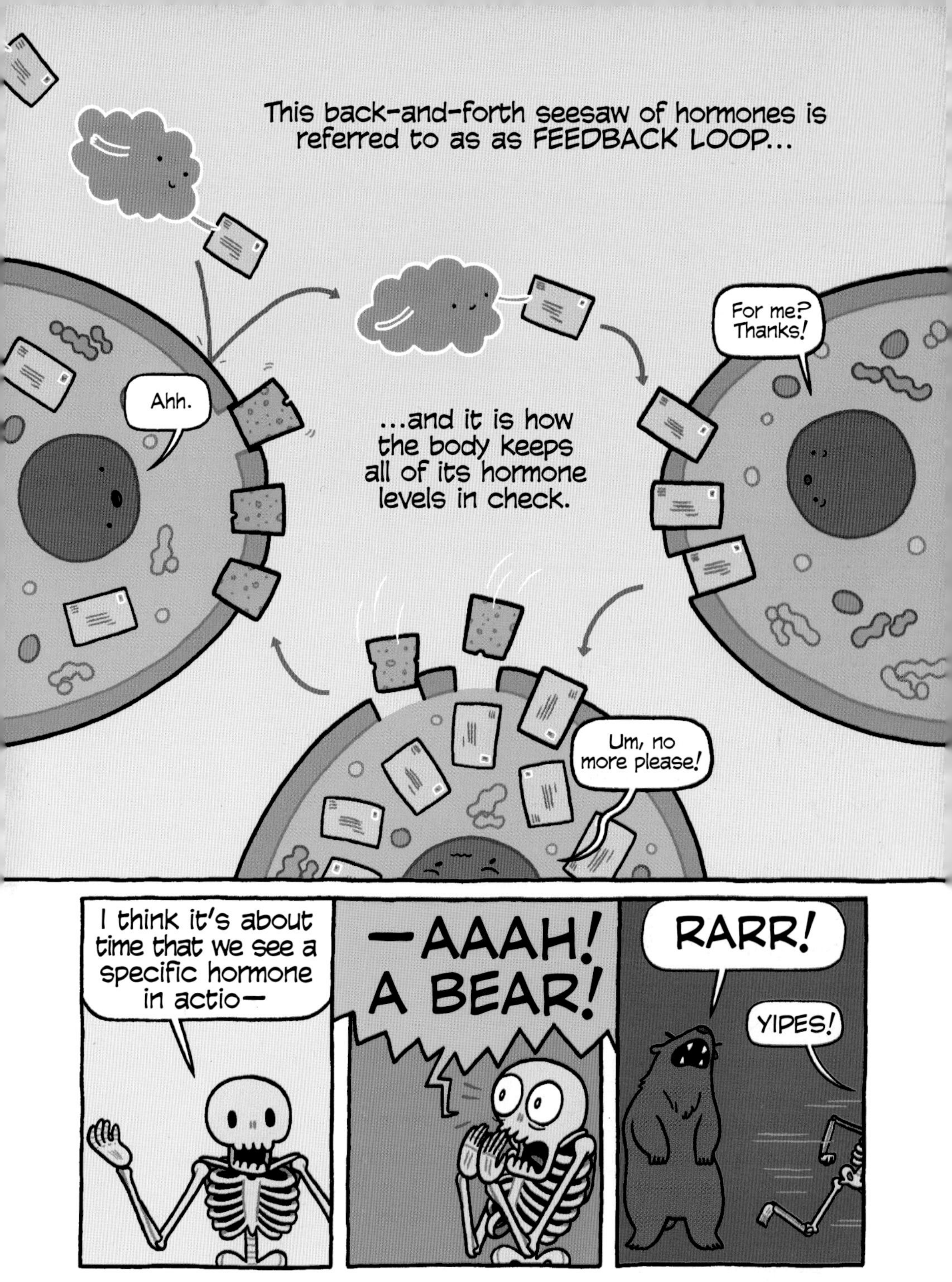
This back-and-forth seesaw of hormones is referred to as as FEEDBACK LOOP...
Ahh.
For me? Thanks!
...and it is how the body keeps all of its hormone levels in check.
Um, no more please!
I think it's about time that we see a specific hormone in actio—
—AAAH! A BEAR!
RARR!
YIPES!

Okay—so, the hormone ADRENALINE just kicked in. My heart is racing, my blood is pumping, and my stomach certainly isn't doing any digesting!

Adrenaline forces my body to focus on simple life-or-death stuff to help me escape danger.

I can keep going—::huff huff::—like this for a little bit...

...but I'm—::huff huff::—using up energy awfully fast!

huff   huff

Me too!

Great job! You scare me every time!

Just doing my job.

Hormones aren't just for getting scared— hormones are responsible for just about anything you can think of:

Stimulating hair growth; causing our skin to darken after sun exposure; reaction to stress, nervousness, or danger...

Remember those "growing pains" from back in the musculatory system?

Well, guess who's in charge of telling those muscles to grow in the first place?

The endocrine system!

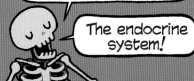

If you are under the age of 25, your pea-sized pituitary gland is hard at work producing hormones to signal growth.

A lot of this work happens at night, while your body is at rest... If you've ever had growing pains, you know that they only happen at night.

Aside from growing taller, there are other physical changes that happen to our bodies as we age.

And the endocrine system is responsible for a major change: PUBERTY.

Puberty is the body's transition from child to adult...

...and some of those changes are different for males and females...

ACT EIGHT:
THE REPRODUCTIVE SYSTEM

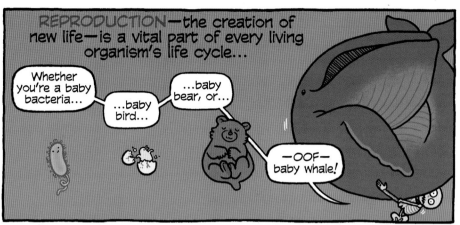

REPRODUCTION—the creation of new life—is a vital part of every living organism's life cycle...

Whether you're a baby bacteria...

...baby bird...

...baby bear, or...

—OOF— baby whale!

GAH!

...and human beings are certainly no exception!

Parents pass on their traits through their genes.

Son, I want you to have these.

?

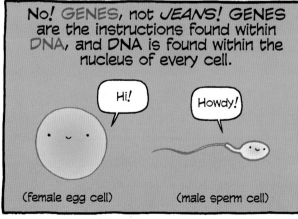

No! GENES, not JEANS! GENES are the instructions found within DNA, and DNA is found within the nucleus of every cell.

Hi!

Howdy!

(female egg cell)

(male sperm cell)

Let's look at the big picture first: REPRODUCTIVE ORGANS can be found in the lower abdomen of both...

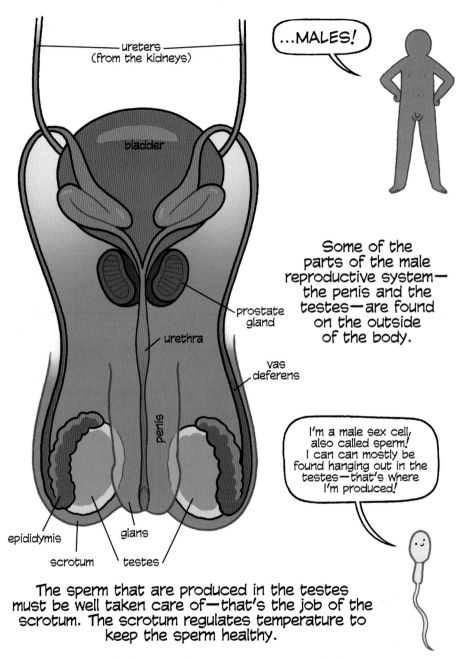

ureters
(from the kidneys)

...MALES!

bladder

Some of the
parts of the male
reproductive system—
the penis and the
testes—are found
on the outside
of the body.

prostate
gland

urethra

vas
deferens

penis

I'm a male sex cell,
also called sperm!
I can can mostly be
found hanging out in the
testes—that's where
I'm produced!

epididymis   glans

scrotum   testes

The sperm that are produced in the testes
must be well taken care of—that's the job of the
scrotum. The scrotum regulates temperature to
keep the sperm healthy.

Too hot and it relaxes to cool off,
and too cold and it contracts to pull the
testes closer to the body to keep warm.

...and
FEMALES!

Almost all the parts of
the female reproductive system are
located on the inside of the body.

The uterus is the stage for...babies!
Its flexible uterine walls can stretch to
accomodate the development of an itty
bitty human being. You might say that
it's a *womb* with a view.

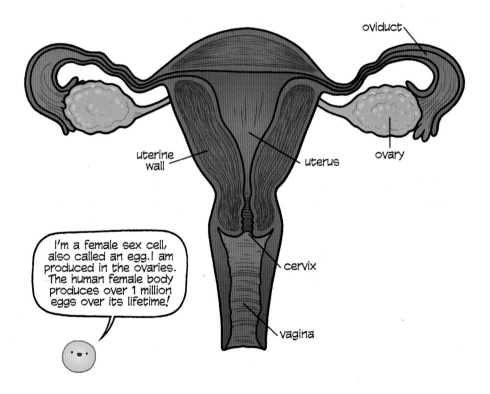

oviduct

uterine
wall

uterus

ovary

I'm a female sex cell,
also called an egg. I am
produced in the ovaries.
The human female body
produces over 1 million
eggs over its lifetime!

cervix

vagina

We'll be exploring the functions of these
two separate systems in this act.

Before we even get to reproduction, we first have to talk about...

PUBERTY

Like I mentioned before...

...puberty marks the beginning of the body's transformation into adulthood.

Hormonal changes, courtesy of the endocrine system...

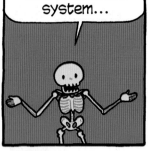

...trigger physical growth, development of the reproductive organs, and changes in behavior.

REPORT FOR PUBERTY TRAINING

hup

hup

hup

hup

hup

Puberty generally begins around ages 10-11 in girls and ages 12-13 in boys.

For both sexes, this usually means rapid growth spurts—

OUCH!

Well, not quite so fast...

—as well as an increase in weight, and emotional changes.

Now, for my next act, I will pull some puberty-specific changes—

—out of my hat!

HAIR!

For both sexes, underarm and pubic hair appear during puberty...

Heeeeeeyyy!

...as well as facial hair for males.

so dignified

Let's see what else we've got...

Blemishes, pimples, and zits, oh my!

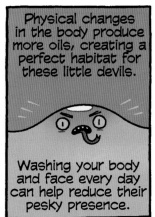

Physical changes in the body produce more oils, creating a perfect habitat for these little devils.

Washing your body and face every day can help reduce their pesky presence.

SNIFF SNIFF

Increased oil production is joined by increased sweat production—resulting in body odor.

Or "BO" for short.

Oop— there's more!

Ah, yes.

Puberty also means breast development for females.

Whew! They just keep coming...

Okay, that seems to be the end.

During puberty, males may experience an increase in muscle bulk and body hair, growth of the reproductive organs, and growth of the larynx (causing the voice to deepen).

TAP
TAP

Females may experience an increase of fat around the hips, as well as the start of menstruation.*

Puberty can definitely be a rough time, but you should know that these types of changes...

...are things that every human being goes through on the road to adulthood.

It is around puberty that people start to become romantically attracted to each other.

EMOTIONS— like sadness or excitement or anger— may feel stronger and this can be confusing.

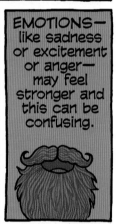

Despite everything going on in your life (and your body), it's important to stay active and try new things.

It's during this time in people's lives that they often form life-long interests...

...so try learning a new instrument, playing a new sport, or taking a challenging class.

*More about menstruation on the next page!

As all these changes during puberty happen, it means that the human body is preparing itself for REPRODUCTION.

This does not mean that as soon as you hit puberty, you have to start having children...

...but once these changes happen, reproduction is possible.

Speaking of reproduction, let's look at one particular change in the female body: menstruation.

Often called a "period," MENSTRUATION begins in females at puberty and continues until menopause (when a female's reproductive system "retires" around the age of 50).

Remember that female egg cell?

Hi again!

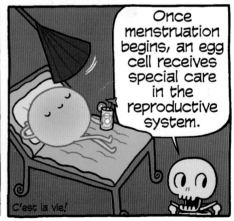

Once menstruation begins, an egg cell receives special care in the reproductive system.

C'est la vie!

LOOKING INSIDE: THE MENSTRUAL CYCLE

Day 1: The menstruation cycle begins! Hormones signal to the uterus to shed its lining of tissue and blood via the vagina. This bleeding lasts about 5 days.

Day 7: Hormones stimulate the production of little fluid-filled "jackets" (called follicles) for some eggs in the ovaries.

Days 7-14: Only one of the follicles continues to develop. Around Day 14, hormones tell that follicle to burst, releasing the egg. This is called OVULATION.

The egg then travels down the oviduct. If it encounters sperm, fertilization may happen. If not, it continues into the uterus, signaling the release of hormones that start menstruation all over again, usually around Day 25.

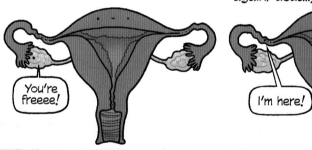

During menstruation, the uterus (which is made of visceral muscles) contracts to move the uterine lining out of the body.

These contractions can be uncomfortable or even painful, and are often referred to as "menstrual cramping" or "cramps."

Women may also experience headaches, nausea, light-headedness, or mood swings around the time of their periods: these are all normal symptoms.

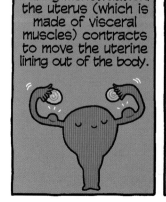

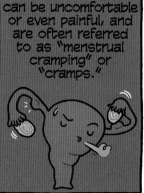

The menstrual cycle takes an average of 28 days, but can be anywhere from 23-35 days.

So organized!

When women first get their periods, they may be irregular, and that's normal.

Just doin' my job.

Let's shift gears and focus on a specific male change. I mentioned earlier that the male reproductive organs enlarge during puberty.

This involves the occurence of erections.

An ERECTION is the stiffening of the penis.

ATTENTION: WOULD SOME BLOOD PLEASE REPORT TO THE PENIS—

—FOR A ROUTINE ERECTION.

The spongy tissue inside the penis fills with blood, causing the penis to enlarge.

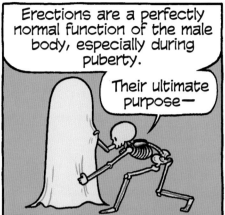

Erections are a perfectly normal function of the male body, especially during puberty.

Their ultimate purpose—

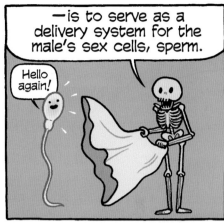

—is to serve as a delivery system for the male's sex cells, sperm.

Hello again!

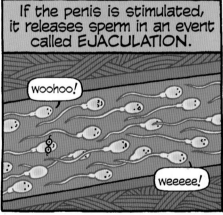

If the penis is stimulated, it releases sperm in an event called EJACULATION.

woohoo!

weeeee!

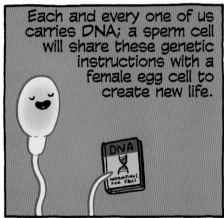

Each and every one of us carries DNA; a sperm cell will share these genetic instructions with a female egg cell to create new life.

DNA

INSTRUCTIONS FOR CELLS

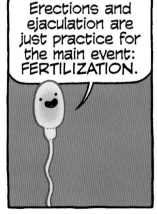

Erections and ejaculation are just practice for the main event: FERTILIZATION.

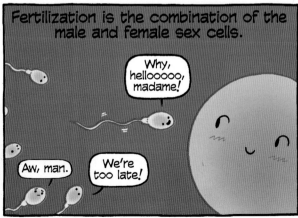

Fertilization is the combination of the male and female sex cells.

Why, hellooooo, madame!

Aw, man.

We're too late!

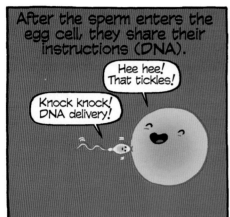

After the sperm enters the egg cell, they share their instructions (DNA).

Hee hee! That tickles!

Knock knock! DNA delivery!

Immediately after fertilization, things begin to happen.

Ooh! I love what you've done with the place!

Why, thank you!

Once the sperm and egg combine...

OH!

...they divide.

1...

2...

And divide again.

...4...

And again.

...8...

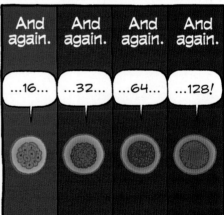

And again.

And again.

And again.

And again.

...16...

...32...

...64...

...128!

Over the course of the next 6 weeks, this clump of dividing cells starts to look more organized.

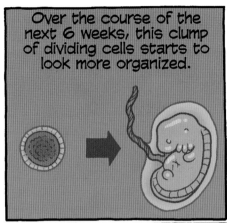

Developing chicken!

Developing bear!

Developing human!

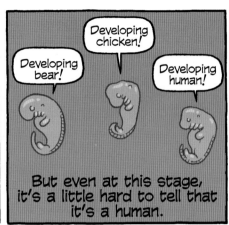

But even at this stage, it's a little hard to tell that it's a human.

Here are some basic milestones in human pregnancy:

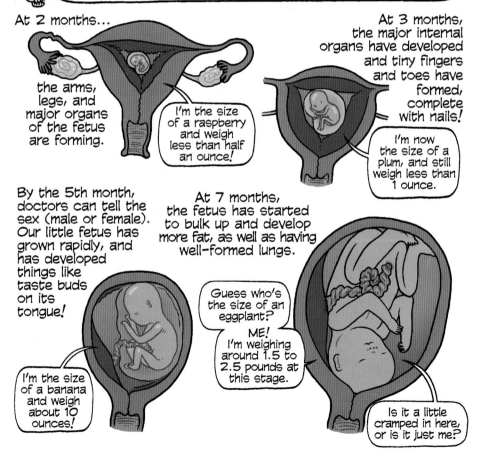

At 2 months...

the arms, legs, and major organs of the fetus are forming.

I'm the size of a raspberry and weigh less than half an ounce!

At 3 months, the major internal organs have developed and tiny fingers and toes have formed, complete with nails!

I'm now the size of a plum, and still weigh less than 1 ounce.

By the 5th month, doctors can tell the sex (male or female). Our little fetus has grown rapidly, and has developed things like taste buds on its tongue!

I'm the size of a banana and weigh about 10 ounces!

At 7 months, the fetus has started to bulk up and develop more fat, as well as having well-formed lungs.

Guess who's the size of an eggplant?

ME! I'm weighing around 1.5 to 2.5 pounds at this stage.

Is it a little cramped in here, or is it just me?

139

You might ask... just how does that baby breathe in there?

Scuba gear? Good guess, but nope!

I don't! Crazy, right?

I share a connection to my mom via this nifty umbilical cord.

It gives me all the nutrients and oxygen that I need.

I'm now roughly the size of a watermelon, and anywhere from 6 to 9 pounds.

I spend a lot of time moving, or trying to move, to stretch my limbs. (Sorry, Mom!)

Yup, it's definitely crowded in here...

...but it's so warm and comfy!

At 9 months, the fetus is fully developed and ready for birth; it may even have hair already! Brain growth has increased these last few weeks, and any other development is preparation for the outside world.

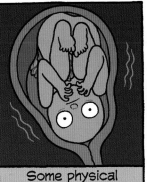

The baby is ready to...debut.

Some physical changes prepare mom and baby for birth.

This is called LABOR, and it is hard work.

TAH-DAH!

Once the baby comes out, the umbilical cord is snipped. What's left of it becomes a belly button.

WAAHHH!

It's cold out here!

Newborn babies can't do all that much, so they need a lot of care.

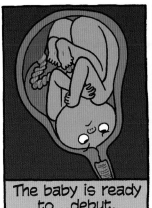

Pregnancy—from fertilization to birth—lasts an average of 266 days; this is called a gestation period.

KITTENZ

Gestation periods are different from mammal to mammal:

A female elephant is pregnant for about 660 days (a little less than 2 years)...

...while a female mouse is pregnant for about 20 days!

Congratulations!

Humans grow the fastest they will ever grow in those first 9 months in the womb.

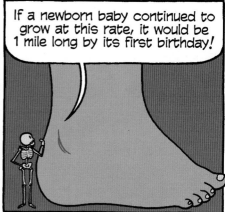

If a newborn baby continued to grow at this rate, it would be 1 mile long by its first birthday!

I mentioned babies needing a lot of care—here are some major baby achievements from the first few years:

By 8 months old, most babies can SIT UP on their own.

A baby can start to have TEETH come in at 6 months (or even earlier) or as late as 18 months.

DAH

OOO

MMM

Babies usually start to CRAWL between 6 and 9 months.

By the time most babies are 12 months old, they can form short words (like "mama" or "dada").

After 4-6 months, a baby is usually ready to start eating SOLID FOOD. These are slowly introduced, then finger foods are added.

Babies generally start to WALK around 9 to 12 months. They start by pulling themselves up and supporting their own weight.

How animals—specifically us humans—care for one another (and ourselves!) has a lot to do with our survival as a species.

This nurturing helps us safely learn, experience the world, and become independent...

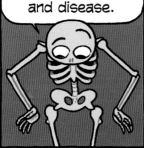

...but our body has its own defense system from infection, illness, and disease.

This role is played by the —ah—AH—

ACT NINE:
THE IMMUNE SYSTEM

Ick.
Excuse me.

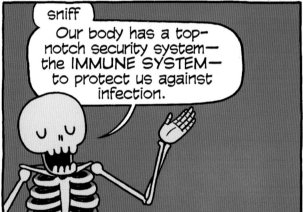

sniff

Our body has a top-notch security system— the IMMUNE SYSTEM— to protect us against infection.

GRRR!

YAH!!

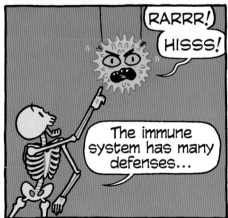

RARRR!

HISSS!

The immune system has many defenses...

OH NO!

...from areas all over the body.

Players for the immune system can be found all over the body (and even in parts of other body systems).

External barriers, like skin, mucus, and hair, help keep infectious organisms from getting into the body.

If germs do make it past these hurdles, the inside of the body is armed with many more fighters.

The lymph system, along with the blood, takes defense cells to where they are needed.

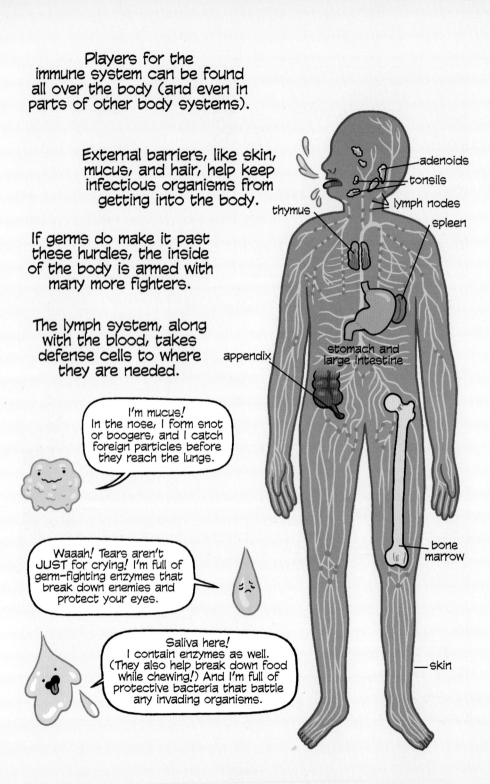

adenoids

tonsils

lymph nodes

spleen

thymus

stomach and large intestine

appendix

bone marrow

skin

I'm mucus! In the nose, I form snot or boogers, and I catch foreign particles before they reach the lungs.

Waaah! Tears aren't JUST for crying! I'm full of germ-fighting enzymes that break down enemies and protect your eyes.

Saliva here! I contain enzymes as well. (They also help break down food while chewing!) And I'm full of protective bacteria that battle any invading organisms.

That's a whole lot of protection.

Let's take a look at what our body is protecting us from.

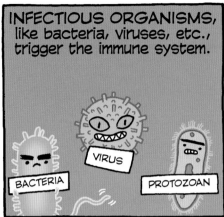

INFECTIOUS ORGANISMS, like bacteria, viruses, etc., trigger the immune system.

BACTERIA

VIRUS

PROTOZOAN

If an infectious organism makes it past those surface barriers—skin, tears, snot, or saliva—the body's next step is either an inflammatory response or an immune response.

HEH HEH

UH-OH

HA HA!

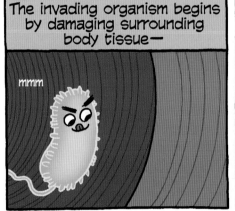

The invading organism begins by damaging surrounding body tissue—

mmm

—it pretty much starts to make a mess.

mmm

om nom nom

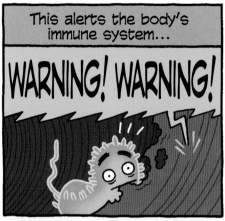

This alerts the body's immune system...

WARNING! WARNING!

...creating an INFLAMMATORY RESPONSE.

Invader detected: activating inflammatory response!

GULP

Uh-oh.

First, the body releases the hormones PROSTAGLANDIN and HISTAMINE.

Their release signals PAIN and SWELLING...

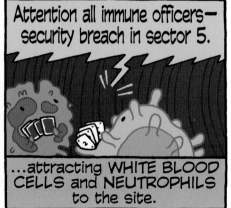

Attention all immune officers— security breach in sector 5.

...attracting WHITE BLOOD CELLS and NEUTROPHILS to the site.

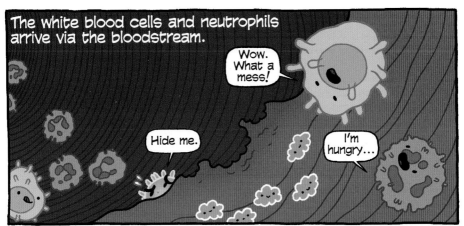

The white blood cells and neutrophils arrive via the bloodstream.

Wow. What a mess!

Hide me.

I'm hungry...

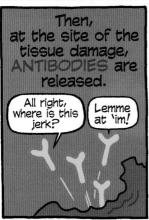

Then, at the site of the tissue damage, ANTIBODIES are released.

All right, where is this jerk?

Lemme at 'im!

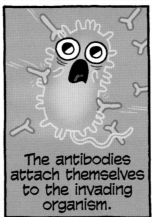

The antibodies attach themselves to the invading organism.

The neutrophils have special receptors just for the antibodies; the two fit together like puzzle pieces.

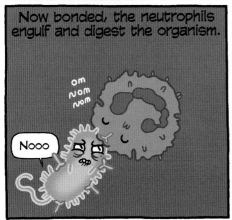

Now bonded, the neutrophils engulf and digest the organism.

om nom nom

Nooo

Once the impostor is broken down, the leftovers are either discarded as waste or stored for future recognition, which brings us to...

BURP!

'scuse me.

149

...IMMUNE RESPONSE.

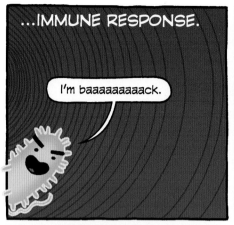

I'm baaaaaaaaack.

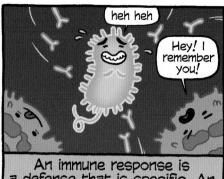

heh heh

Hey! I remember you!

An immune response is a defense that is specific. An infectious organsim is targeted with special antibodies.

If the body stores antibodies from a previous infection, it can use these antibodies for a quicker, more precise attack.

Welcome to the GERM LIBRARY

A - L

m - z

An immune response may also be used if an initial inflammatory response fails.

Welcome to the GERM LIBRARY

A - L

m - z

Let's take another look at your immune system in action.

I'll need a volunteer...

...to help demonstrate LOCAL INFECTION.

UGH. Not AGAIN.

A local infection occurs superficially, meaning on the skin and other areas of the outside of the body.

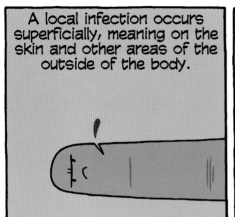

The body reacts just like it did for the inflammatory response, but a few other things happen.

YIPES!

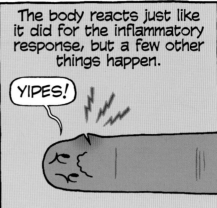

LOOKING INSIDE: LOCAL INFECTION

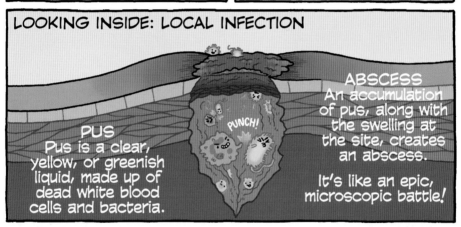

PUNCH!

PUS
Pus is a clear, yellow, or greenish liquid, made up of dead white blood cells and bacteria.

ABSCESS
An accumulation of pus, along with the swelling at the site, creates an abscess.

It's like an epic, microscopic battle!

Our bodies already have a pretty good defense when it comes to infections.

The best thing you can do is keep the infected area clean and dry.

Usually, your body will heal itself on its own.

Sometimes if an infection won't go away, gets worse, or is near a senstive area (like the eyes), you may need to see a doctor.

And they might give you medicine to help you to heal.

Thanks, finger. You're the best!

Aw, shucks.

It was nothin'.

Okay, so it's obvious we've got a great defense system.

Now let's get up close and personal with all these tiny terrors.

Ladies and gentlemen, I present to you—

—the chorus line of infectious organisms!

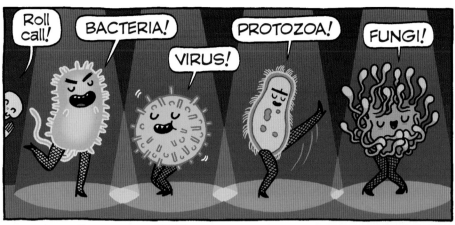

Roll call!

BACTERIA!

VIRUS!

PROTOZOA!

FUNGI!

Um...

...I'll...I'll just be...over here...

Take it away!

Ahem...

BACTERIA are single-celled organisms that are present in air, soil, water...even animals!

We're...pretty much everywhere.

But don't worry, not all of us are harmful.

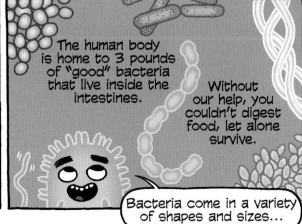

The human body is home to 3 pounds of "good" bacteria that live inside the intestines.

Without our help, you couldn't digest food, let alone survive.

Bacteria come in a variety of shapes and sizes...

153

...and can cause infections such as:

STREP

I inflame your throat and tonsils!

TETANUS

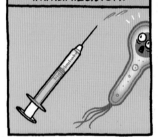

I can be found on rusty or dirty objects, and I create a dangerous infection that affects your muscles.

Lucky for humans, there is a vaccine that prevents infections from me.

STAPH

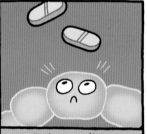

My family and I can cause everything from food poisoning to conjunctivitis to skin infections.

Infections from some bacteria (like tetanus) can be prevented by immunization.

Others (like strep throat) can be treated with medicines called ANTIBIOTICS.

A lot of the time, the body's immune system is the best defense against invading bacteria.

Bacteria cause damage to the body in two ways: by invading and destroying tissue cells...

mmmmm

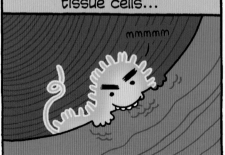

...and/or producing poisonous substances called TOXINS.

TOOT!

Now, I probably shouldn't be telling you this, but...here are some common bacteria as well as ways to prevent them:

CAVITIES!

That's right, cavities are caused by sugar-loving bacteria. The more sugar you eat, the more fuel you're providing for these little guys to eat away at your teeth!

Staph bacteria (aka staphylococcus) can be found on the skin, and if they enter a cut, they can cause an infection. If staph bacteria get inside the body, they can cause a far worse infection.

STAPH!

SALMONELLA!

and E. COLI!

Salmonella and E. coli are 2 different bacteria, but they both can cause gastrointestinal trouble. Cooking meat to the correct temperature and washing fruits and veggies can prevent these two bacteria from getting into your body.

You're a bunch of little stinkers, aren't ya?

HEY! We're not ALL bad...

You should check out VIRUSES, though... they're always bad news!

HEH HEH

I am a very small infectious organism that can only live inside of another organism.

In this case—YOU!

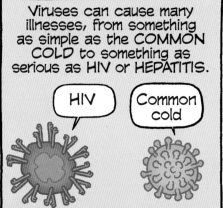

Viruses can cause many illnesses, from something as simple as the COMMON COLD to something as serious as HIV or HEPATITIS.

HIV

Common cold

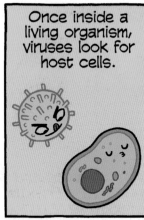

Once inside a living organism, viruses look for host cells.

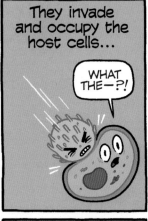

They invade and occupy the host cells...

WHAT THE—?!

...using them for nutrients and energy...

I don't feel so good...

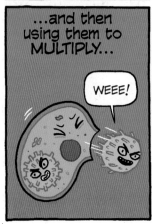

...and then using them to MULTIPLY...

WEEE!

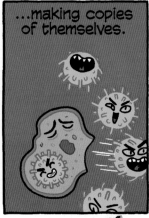

...making copies of themselves.

This continues until the host cell either dies or loses the ability to function normally.

Some viruses can be treated with medicine, but a lot of the time, your immune system does all the work.

And, just like some bacteria, some viruses can be avoided through immunization.

 Here are some other ailments and illnesses, and a look at the viruses that cause them:

Over 200 different viruses are responsible for what we call the COMMON COLD.

GASTROENTERITIS and ROTA- and NOROVIRUSES

 We'll make you poop...

...and/or puke!

WARTS

Warts are caused by the HPV (human papillomavirus), and there are over 130 different types of these viruses.

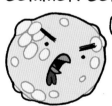 ba-GAWK!

CHICKEN POX is caused by the varicella-zoster virus, and it is a common infection, especially in kids under 12.

INFLUENZA (aka the FLU)

I'll make you feel terrible.

MUMPS!

MEASLES!

RUBELLA!

These three viruses are prevented by a common vaccine... sorry, fellas!

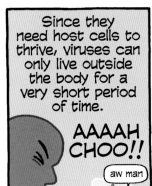

Since they need host cells to thrive, viruses can only live outside the body for a very short period of time.

AAAAH CHOO!!

aw man

If you avoid sharing food and drinks, and wash your hands before and after you eat—

Sharing is not always caring.

mmm-hmmm

—you can reduce your risk of getting invaded by viruses.

Here lies poor virus: it could not find a host cell.

Sometimes I'm pretty hard to avoid—you've had a cold before, right?

But PROTOZOANS are a little bit easier to keep out of your life.

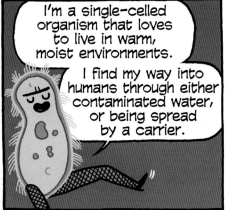

I'm a single-celled organism that loves to live in warm, moist environments.

I find my way into humans through either contaminated water, or being spread by a carrier.

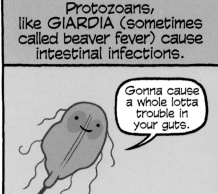

Protozoans, like GIARDIA (sometimes called beaver fever) cause intestinal infections.

Gonna cause a whole lotta trouble in your guts.

Giardia is found in streams, ponds, lakes, or swamps, so an easy way to avoid it is to drink clean water.

Psst, drink this pond water!

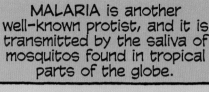

MALARIA is another well-known protist, and it is transmitted by the saliva of mosquitos found in tropical parts of the globe.

Hey, don't blame me.

Luckily, there are ways to prevent and treat this illness.

There's someone else here who enjoys warm, moist environments...

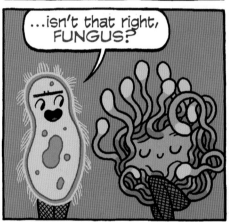

...isn't that right, FUNGUS?

Oh, yes!

Us fungi loooooove dark, wet places.

Mushrooms are one kind of fungi...

'sup

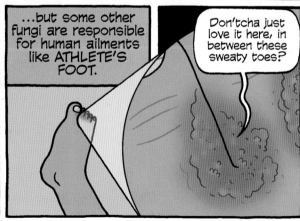

...but some other fungi are responsible for human ailments like ATHLETE'S FOOT.

Don'tcha just love it here, in between these sweaty toes?

All fungi are simple organisms that scavenge dead or rotting tissue.

In this case, I'm chowing down on your dead skin cells.

NUM
NUM
NUM
MMM
YUM
OM
NUM

Fungal infections usually happen on the outside of the body in the hair, skin, or nails, or around mucus membranes like the nose, eyes, and mouth.

Keeping your body clean by regularly washing with soap and warm water...

...or using an anti-fungal medication or treated powder to dry out the affected area...

...will help keep fungi out of your life.

sob!

I've got nowhere to live!

So...that's all of us!

There, there.

Remember when we mentioned there's a way to prevent some bacterial and viral infections?

It's through the use of IMMUNIZATION!!

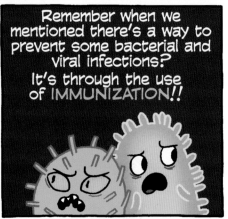

Did somebody say my name?

AH!

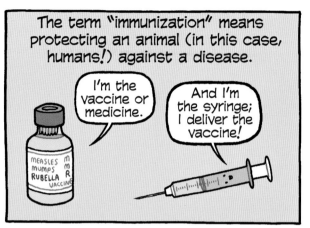

The term "immunization" means protecting an animal (in this case, humans!) against a disease.

I'm the vaccine or medicine.

And I'm the syringe; I deliver the vaccine!

MEASLES
MUMPS
RUBELLA
VACCINE
M M R

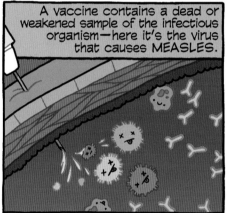

A vaccine contains a dead or weakened sample of the infectious organism—here it's the virus that causes MEASLES.

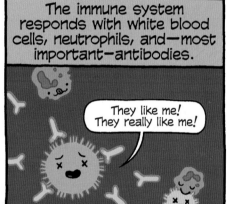

The immune system responds with white blood cells, neutrophils, and—most important—antibodies.

They like me! They really like me!

The body creates specific antibodies for measles, which are stored away...

Welcome to the GERM LIBRARY

A-L

M-Z

...where they'll be called into action if the body is ever exposed to the measles virus.

BRING IT ON!!

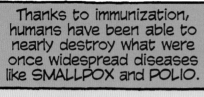

Thanks to immunization, humans have been able to nearly destroy what were once widespread diseases like SMALLPOX and POLIO.

Just doin' my job... thank YOU, scientists who developed me!

So even though shots might not feel that great...

...remember that these vaccinations help to protect us against some serious sicknesses!

Our immune system is pretty amazing, huh?

Well, there might be some exceptions...

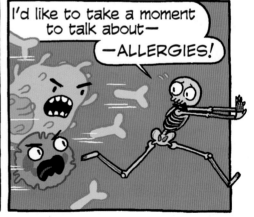

I'd like to take a moment to talk about—

—ALLERGIES!

Is it all clear?

Okay, as I was *trying* to say...

An ALLERGY is an inappropriately strong immune response to something that's pretty harmless.

These substances are called ALLERGENS—remember some of them from the respiratory system?

3 IN

2.5 IN

...UST

ANIMAL HAIR

MOLD

CIGARETTE SMOKE

Well, that's not all of them. Allergens can be INHALED, INGESTED, or EXPOSED to the eyes or skin.

Here are some common culprits:

DAIRY PRODUCTS

BEE STINGS

PEANUTS

BANANAS (& LATEX)

MILK 2%

SHELLFISH

TREE POLLEN

Here's what goes on inside the body during an ALLERGIC REACTION.

We'll use PEANUTS as the allergen. Once the allergen is inside of the body, it sets off a chain reaction.

doo dee doo...

...just hangin' out in here.

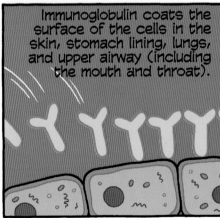

WARNING! WARNING! ALLERGEN DETECTED!

This can't be good...

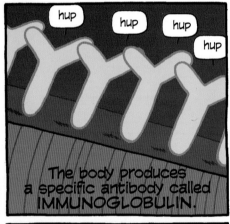

hup

hup

hup

hup

The body produces a specific antibody called IMMUNOGLOBULIN.

Immunoglobulin coats the surface of the cells in the skin, stomach lining, lungs, and upper airway (including the mouth and throat).

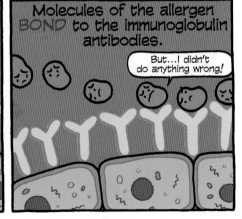

Molecules of the allergen BOND to the immunoglobulin antibodies.

But...I didn't do anything wrong!

This bonding signals the release of the inflammatory hormones PROSTAGLANDIN and HISTAMINE—

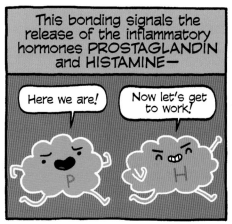

Here we are!

Now let's get to work!

Ugh. I feel TERRIBLE.

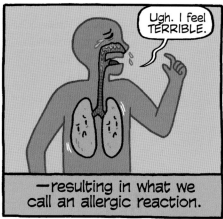

—resulting in what we call an allergic reaction.

These symptoms affect the areas of the body covered in immunoglobulin, and that's why allergies are usually charactized by...

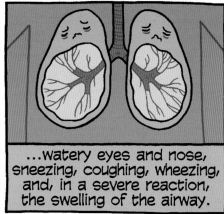

...watery eyes and nose, sneezing, coughing, wheezing, and, in a severe reaction, the swelling of the airway.

If a person knows that they have a severe allergy, they might carry a device called an auto-injector.

Here I am, at your service!

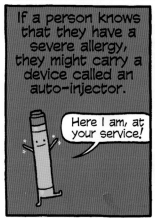

CLICK

If there's a severe reaction, the auto-injector can be used to deliver a quick dose of EPINEPHRINE* via a needle.

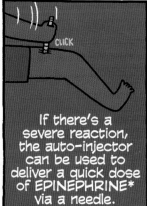

This medicine will usually relax the person's airways, but they still need to go to the hospital afterward to be checked out.

*another name for the hormone ADRENALINE

The best way to avoid an allergic reaction is to avoid the allergen, but that's not always so easy.

For milder allergies, there are medicines that help reduce allergy symptoms.

Sometimes your doctor might even expose you to small amounts of the allergen to help your body get used to it.

Just a teeny, tiny bit!

It's often unclear why we develop allergies.

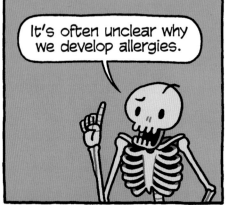

achoo

ACHOO

Sometimes people get them when they are young; others develop them later in life.

Sometimes allergies actually disapper!

Well...

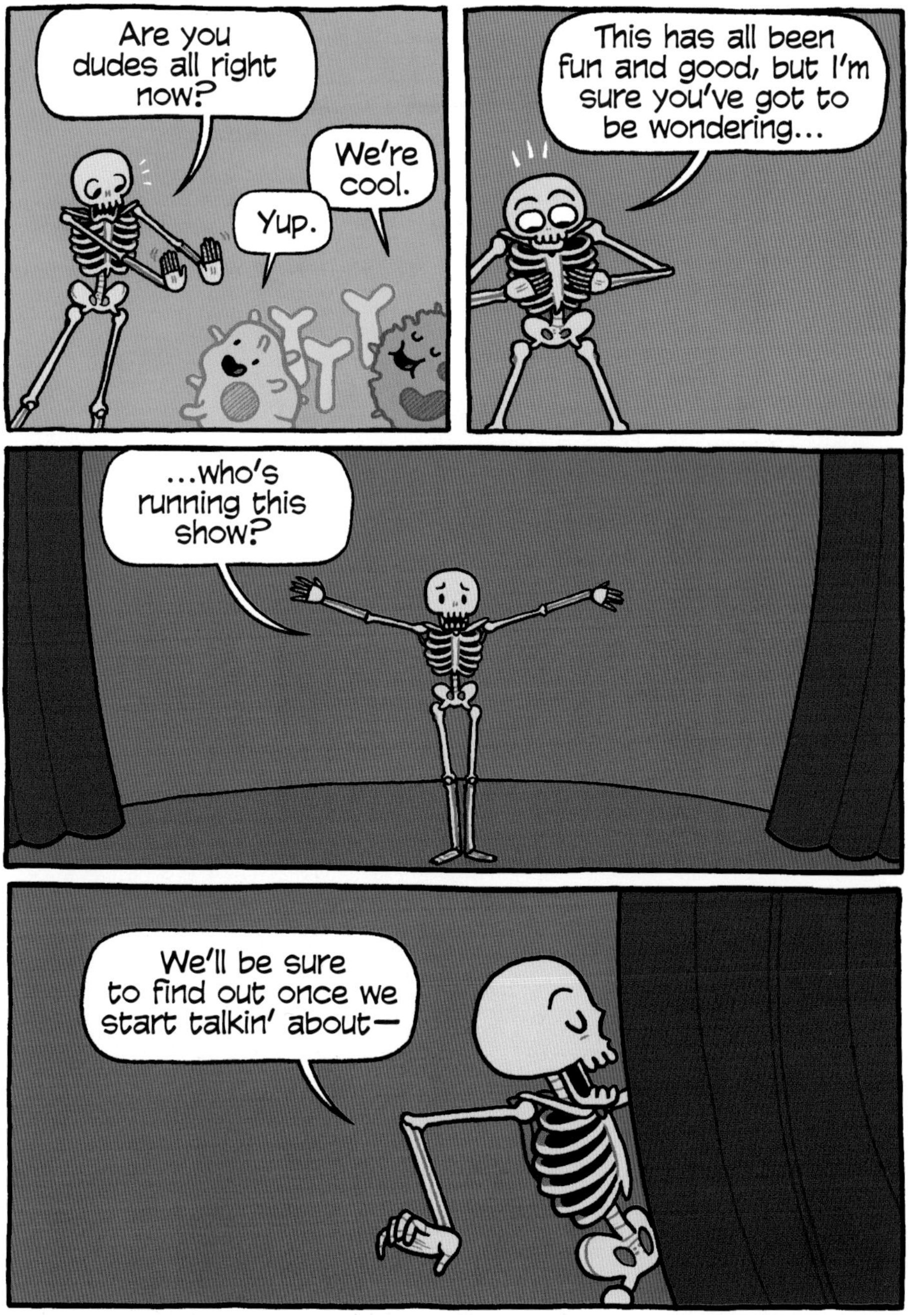
Are you dudes all right now?
We're cool.
Yup.
This has all been fun and good, but I'm sure you've got to be wondering...
...who's running this show?
We'll be sure to find out once we start talkin' about—

BRAINS!

ACT TEN:
THE NERVOUS SYSTEM

Our brains are part of the NERVOUS SYSTEM.

SQUISHY SQUISH

The nervous system governs both CONSCIOUS THOUGHT...

...and everyday INVOLUNTARY ACTIONS.

Oops.

SPLAT

heh heh

I'll just, uh, clean this off a bit...

BRUSH BRUSH

In the animal kingdon, brains range from the size of a beach ball (blue whale) to a simple network of nerve cells (jellyfish).

Let's take a look at ALL the parts of the human nervous system and see what they do.

The brain is connected to the rest of the body through the spinal cord and nerves.

Nerves, in turn, pass along sensory messages to and from areas near and far.

Shown here are only a few of the specific nerves in the human body; there are LOTS more. Just as the arteries and veins carry blood, nerves carry messages.

Our nervous system allows us to sense pain and pleasure, move fast and slow, read and write and talk, chew and swallow and digest...

...whether it's a direct command from the brain or an involuntary response from our network of nerves.

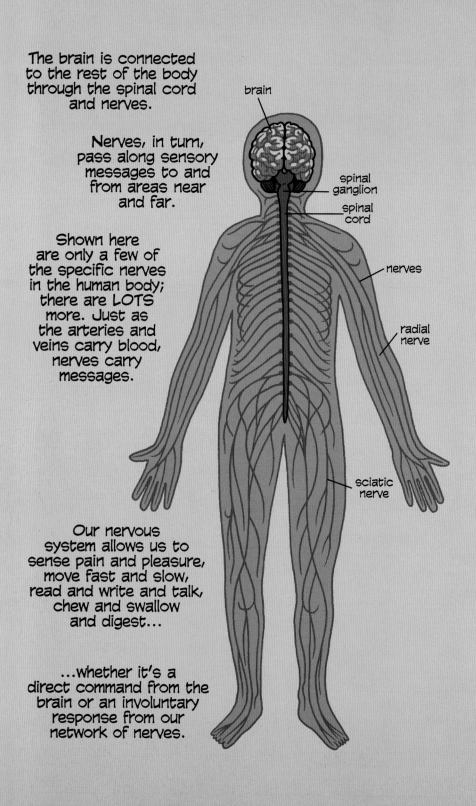

brain

spinal ganglion

spinal cord

nerves

radial nerve

sciatic nerve

Oh, thank you.

The nervous system delivers A LOT of messages.

You want to move your foot?

Your nervous system has to pass that command from your brain to your foot.

Ah-hah!

This is a letter from my brain to remind me to first talk about nerve cells— NEURONS!

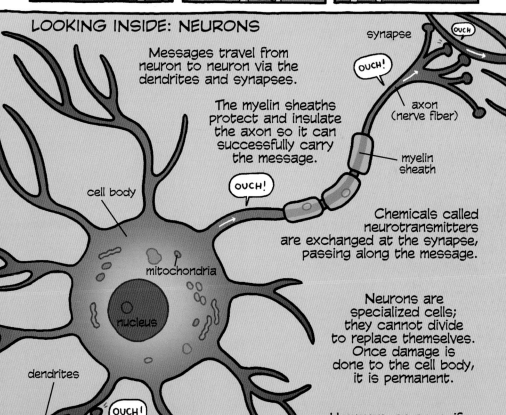

LOOKING INSIDE: NEURONS

Messages travel from neuron to neuron via the dendrites and synapses.

The myelin sheaths protect and insulate the axon so it can successfully carry the message.

synapse

OUCH

OUCH!

axon (nerve fiber)

myelin sheath

OUCH!

cell body

mitochondria

nucleus

dendrites

OUCH!

Chemicals called neurotransmitters are exchanged at the synapse, passing along the message.

Neurons are specialized cells; they cannot divide to replace themselves. Once damage is done to the cell body, it is permanent.

However, an axon, if damaged, can rebuild and repair itself and its myelin sheaths.

Neurons are bundled together within NERVES...

...and there are over 30,000 miles (50,000 kilometers) of nerves in a single human body.

Here's a look at how those nerves send and receive information.

And for this demonstration, we'll be using everybody's favorite guinea pig: Finger!

Nerves in the skin can sense pain, as well as pressure and temperature.

I hate you.

Neurons respond to a stimulus, and send out an electrical impulse.

OUCH!

POKE!

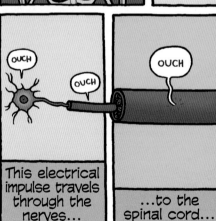

OUCH

OUCH

This electrical impulse travels through the nerves...

OUCH

...to the spinal cord...

OUCH

...and then on to the brain.

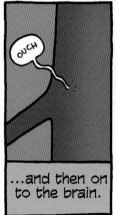

OUCH!

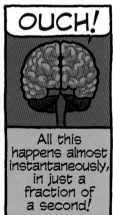

All this happens almost instantaneously, in just a fraction of a second!

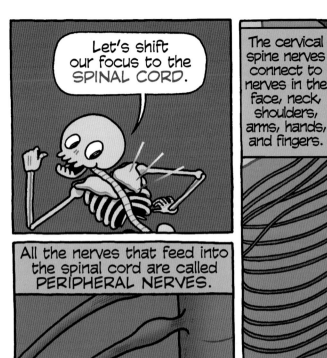

Let's shift our focus to the SPINAL CORD.

All the nerves that feed into the spinal cord are called PERIPHERAL NERVES.

Their job is to carry messages to and from the far reaches of the body.

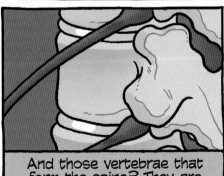

And those vertebrae that form the spine? They are specially shaped to protect the spinal cord.

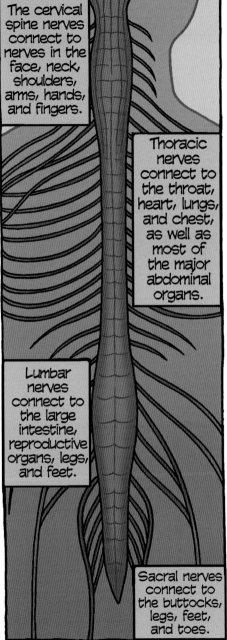

The cervical spine nerves connect to nerves in the face, neck, shoulders, arms, hands, and fingers.

Thoracic nerves connect to the throat, heart, lungs, and chest, as well as most of the major abdominal organs.

Lumbar nerves connect to the large intestine, reproductive organs, legs, and feet.

Sacral nerves connect to the buttocks, legs, feet, and toes.

The spinal cord is split up into sections that are responsible for the involuntary actions of the internal organs and body parts.

This command network is known as the AUTONOMIC NERVOUS SYSTEM.

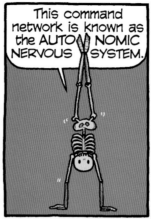

The autonomic nervous system (or ANS for short) has two roles:

The "fight-or-flight" response and the "rest-and-digest" response.

Usually, our body is in rest-and-digest mode, and it operates our organs in a normal way.

ah

These functions are run by a part of the ANS called the parasympathetic nervous system; your heart beats at its regular pace and your digestive system does its job...digesting.

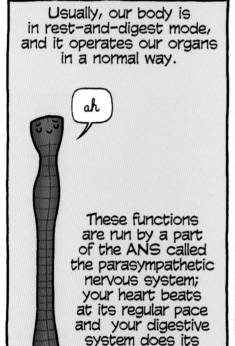

In an emergency, our body switches to fight-or-flight mode; this helps us defend ourselves, or run away from danger.

AAH!

When we are in danger, a part of the ANS called the sympathetic nervous system steps up to the plate; your heart rate increases, digestion slows, and your body prepares to defend itself (or run away)!

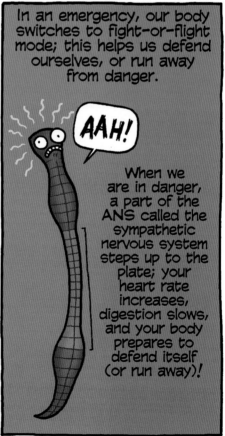

And just like the involuntary actions it oversees, the autonomic nervous system is also involuntary.

You don't have to think to make your heart beat, stomach digest, or lungs breathe.

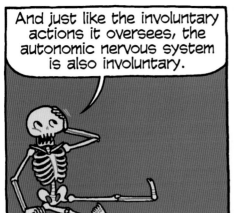

On the topic of *thinking*...I think it's about time we introduced the "motherboard," the "big kahuna," the...

BRAIN!

Made of over 12 billion neurons, the brain has a ton of jobs. For one, it works with the spinal cord to monitor and regulate involuntary bodily functions.

But the brain also controls voluntary actions—if you want to wave your arm or wiggle your toes, those commands come straight from the brain.

Perhaps the most important duty is the brain's role in CONSCIOUSNESS and INTELLECTUAL FUNCTIONS.

PAT PAT

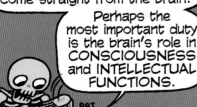

The brain allows us to think, feel, invent, and create!

Whew! I'm getting ahead of myself. First, let's look at the parts of the brain...

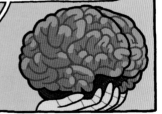

THE OUTER BRAIN

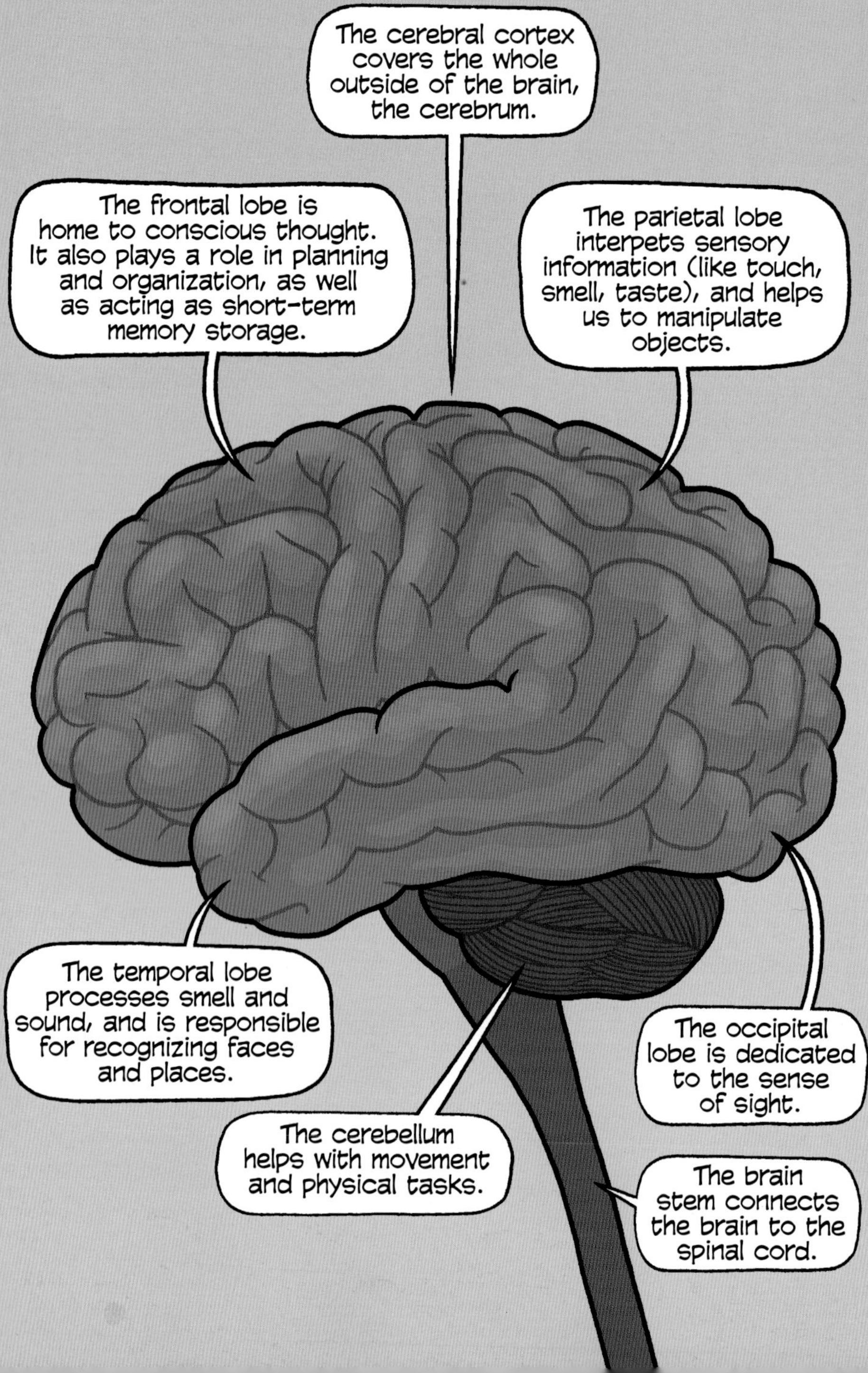

THE INNER BRAIN

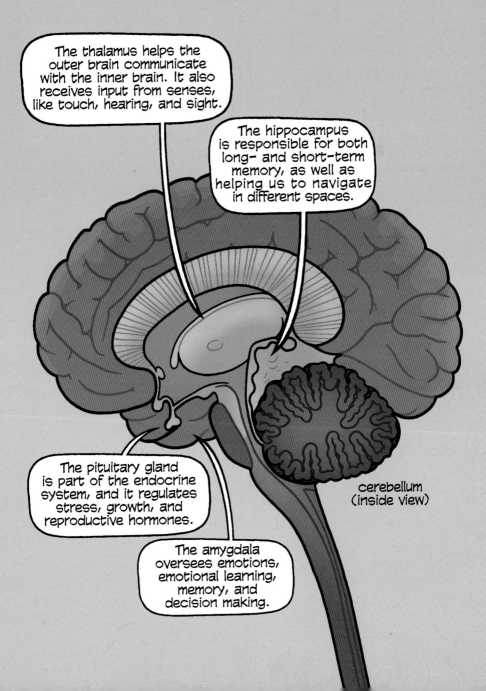

The thalamus helps the outer brain communicate with the inner brain. It also receives input from senses, like touch, hearing, and sight.

The hippocampus is responsible for both long- and short-term memory, as well as helping us to navigate in different spaces.

The pituitary gland is part of the endocrine system, and it regulates stress, growth, and reproductive hormones.

The amygdala oversees emotions, emotional learning, memory, and decision making.

cerebellum (inside view)

There are A LOT of actions that the brain controls:

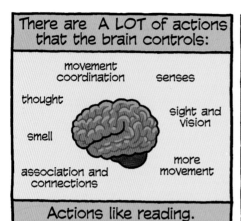

movement coordination

senses

thought

smell

sight and vision

association and connections

more movement

Actions like reading.

It probably doesn't feel like work to read these words, but you should know that your brain is busy at work, making sense of the words (and pictures) to interpret what I'm saying.

Hmm... It says here that you're not just reading each word...

...but also stringing them together to form whole sentences, whole chapters...

whoa.

So, how did we learn this whole "reading" thing in the first place?

Ah-HAH!

MEMORY.

The brain stores all different types of memories—everything from where you put your keys...

...to how to do long division...

...to the smell of your favorite cookies baking.

Back to reading— do you remember when you started learning to read? Probably not, because it started with ...

BOX O' MEMORIES

...learning letters and numbers...

...then the alphabet...

...and then some words...

...and more words.

BOX O' MEMORIES

HUMAN BODY THEATER

All this time, you were learning to speak and write as well.

Learning, memory, thinking—the more you do all of these things, the more connections your brain makes, the better it gets it gets for your brain (and you)!

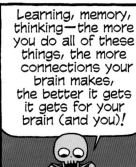

Take a good look at these objects:

Now turn the page.

Without looking at the previous page, see if you can remember all of the objects. *Extra points* if you remember* where *they go.*

? ? ? ?

? ? ? ?

? ? ? ?

How did you do?

Memory games like that are like push-ups for your brain!

Just like every other system in the body, it is important to keep your nervous system healthy.

Here are some ways to keep your brain-engine tuned up and running:

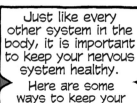

SLEEP is our body's natural way of recharging its "batteries."

Our heart never stops beating, our stomach never stops digesting, and our lungs never stop breathing...

...and our neurons never stop firing. But without sleep, our body cannot function.

DREAMS are a great example of the brain's activity during sleep!

Eating healthy is good for the whole body, and the brain needs nutrients to work best, too.

Eating regular meals is also important— if you've ever skipped a meal or forgotten breakfast, you've felt the consequences.

Mmm... brain foods.

*I lied. There are no points at all—this ain't a quiz!

EXERCISE!

HUFF HUFF

I don't mean jumping jacks (but, of course, those are fine to do).

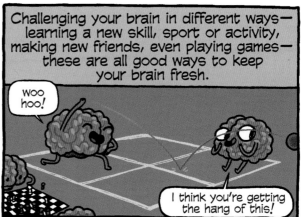

Challenging your brain in different ways—learning a new skill, sport or activity, making new friends, even playing games—these are all good ways to keep your brain fresh.

WOO hoo!

I think you're getting the hang of this!

HELMETS!

This may seem like a no-brainer (ha!), but physically protecting your brain and spinal cord is important, too!

Our body comes with its own bone-y "helmet"—thanks, skull—but if you are participating in an activity or sport that has a risk of impact, wearing a helmet can prevent injury to the head and neck.

KNOCK KNOCK

Even when we take top-notch care of our brains, they can still give us a...

HEADACHE!!

Headaches are not actually a pain in the brain.

Believe it or not, the brain can't actually feel pain because it lacks the pain-sensing neurons found elsewhere in the body.

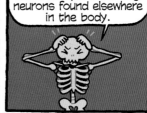

Headaches are usually caused by the blood vessels in the head and neck.

TENSION headaches are caused by the head and neck muscles squeezing too hard, usually as a result of stress.

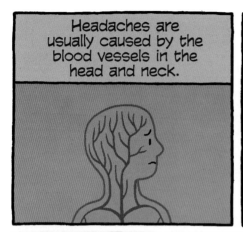

EYESTRAIN, often caused by looking too long at a television or computer screen, can be another headache inducer...

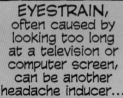

heh heh... I guess I should take a break...

...as well as DEHYDRATION.

So drink that water.

sassy hydration pose

All of these things can cause a dull ache in the head and neck.

A MIGRAINE is a more severe headache, characterized by sharp, throbbing pain in the head, sensitivty to light, dizziness, and nausea.

Headaches can be caused by LOTS of other things:

They can be a symptom of another illness (like a cold, or the flu)...

...lack of sleep or exhaustion...

I'VE BEEN AWAKE FOR 24 HOURS!!

...caffeine (a substance found in coffee, tea, and some sodas)...

SLURPP!

...and stress.

I have a test in EVERY subject tomorrow?!

Whew! Here are some ways to PREVENT headaches:

drink plenty of water

rest after vigorous activities

get plenty of sleep

reduce eyestrain by limiting computer/TV

remember to wear glasses if you need them

consider sporting some sunglasses if you are out in the sun for a long time

If you already have a headache, here are some ways to help recover:

Get plenty of rest or sleep—in a dark, quiet room if you can.

Drink water.

People might take medicine (like a pain reliever) to help get rid of a headache...

...but check with an adult or doctor first.

This body is starting to feel pretty good!

You're welcome.

We've spent so much time looking at what's on the INSIDE...I think it's about time we looked at the OUTSIDE, or rather, how we EXPERIENCE the outside world.

It's time for us to use our—

ACT ELEVEN:
SMELL, TASTE, HEARING, SIGHT, and TOUCH

We interact with and experience our surroundings through our 5 SENSES.

Each one of them helps us to survive—

—ICK.

Smell.

Taste.

Hearing.

Sight.

Touch.

Our senses...

...allow us to feel pain...

HOT!

SMOKE!

...keep us safe...

...warn us of danger...

FIRE!

YUM!

...even permit us to feel pleasure.

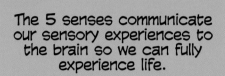

And here's the location of these senses:

The 5 senses communicate our sensory experiences to the brain so we can fully experience life.

Images are viewed by the eye and passed on to the brain to be interpreted.

When we inhale, molecules in the air pass through the nose, where smell cells receive those molecules.

Those flappy things on either side of your head—ears—are specially shaped to catch sounds and funnel them into your inner ear, where they are relayed to the brain.

Texture, temperature, pain, and pressure are detected by sensory nerves in the skin.

Taste and smell work as a team, but taste still does some work on its own. Molecules in the mouth are recognized by taste buds.

sniff
sniff

POP
POP
POP

POP POP
POP
POP
POP
POP

Mmm...

Delicious!

You just witnessed ALL of my senses at work!

I want to talk about SMELL and TASTE.

These 2 senses work together in perfect harmony—

—they are quite the team.

GOOD

NOT SO GOOD

Smell and taste allow us to enjoy food, but also alert us to dangers, like spoiled food or smoke.

Also called CHEMOSENSES, smell and taste monitor food and drink going into the digestive system.

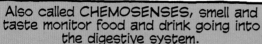

None shall pass!

Unless we say so!

HALT!

Poisonous, rotten, or even just plain unfamiliar food and drink may have a foul smell or unpleasant taste.

This cautions the body against potentially dangerous foods.

I dunno... They smell kinda funny.

Eh, let's give 'em a try.

All right, you may pass.

WOO-HOO!

But just because YOU might think Brussels sprouts taste bad, it DOES NOT mean that they are poisonous.

Our sense of smell alone acts as an early warning system for the respiratory system.

Now let me tell you how I work!

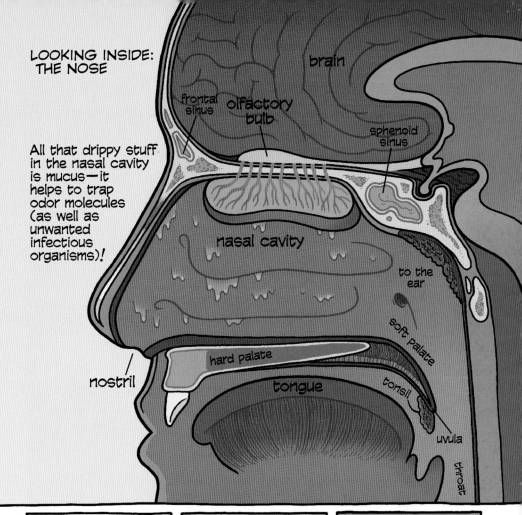

LOOKING INSIDE: THE NOSE

brain

frontal sinus

olfactory bulb

sphenoid sinus

All that drippy stuff in the nasal cavity is mucus—it helps to trap odor molecules (as well as unwanted infectious organisms)!

nasal cavity

to the ear

soft palate

nostril

hard palate

tongue

tonsil

uvula

throat

As you know, everything on this planet is made of atoms.

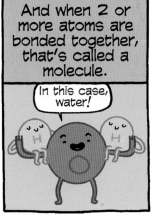

And when 2 or more atoms are bonded together, that's called a molecule.

In this case, water!

And I'm hydrogen sulfide—aka "rotten egg smell"!

189

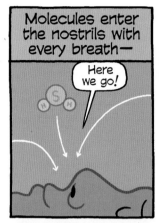

Molecules enter the nostrils with every breath—

Here we go!

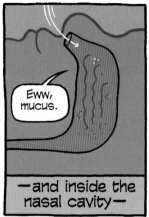

Eww, mucus.

—and inside the nasal cavity—

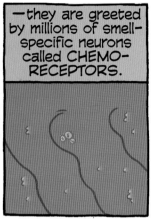

—they are greeted by millions of smell-specific neurons called CHEMO-RECEPTORS.

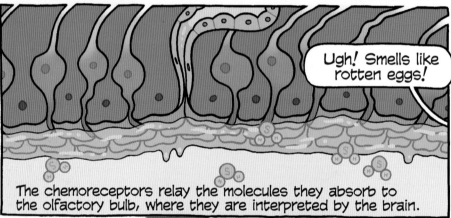

Ugh! Smells like rotten eggs!

The chemoreceptors relay the molecules they absorb to the olfactory bulb, where they are interpreted by the brain.

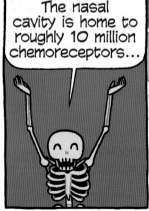

The nasal cavity is home to roughly 10 million chemoreceptors...

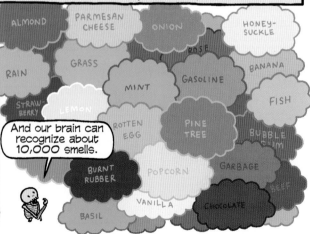

And our brain can recognize about 10,000 smells.

ALMOND
PARMESAN CHEESE
ONION
HONEY-SUCKLE
RAIN
GRASS
ROSE
BANANA
GASOLINE
MINT
STRAW-BERRY
LEMON
FISH
ROTTEN EGG
PINE TREE
BUBBLE GUM
BURNT RUBBER
POPCORN
GARBAGE
VANILLA
CHOCOLATE
BASIL

BASIL BANANA
CHEESE
POPCORN STRAW-BERRY
BACON ONION
FISH
VANILLA
MINT CHOCO

Notice how many of these smells are from food?

Let's take a look at TASTE.

Well, it's about time!

in order to do that, we must say —

AAAAAAHHHH.

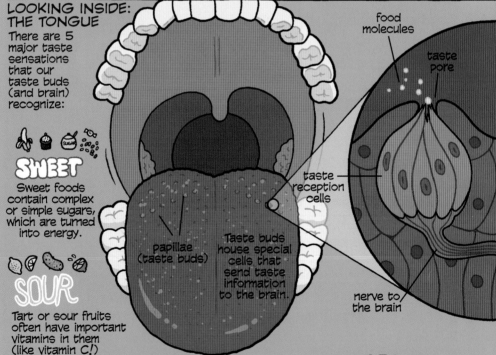

LOOKING INSIDE: THE TONGUE

There are 5 major taste sensations that our taste buds (and brain) recognize:

SWEET

Sweet foods contain complex or simple sugars, which are turned into energy.

SOUR

Tart or sour fruits often have important vitamins in them (like vitamin C!)

SALTY

Salt is a taste enhancer; it can intensify the flavors in food.

papillae (taste buds)

Taste buds house special cells that send taste information to the brain.

food molecules

taste pore

taste reception cells

nerve to the brain

Bitter tastes can warn us of unripe or inedible foods, but also are present in food like chocolate.

BITTER

UMAMI

Umami, or savory, tastes are associated with meats, cheeses, mushrooms, and soy sauce.

Those PAPILLAE (taste buds) that cover the tongue work nonstop when we eat and drink.

We're buds.

Best buds.

In addition to flavors, they sense temperature—

TOO HOT!

—and spiciness—

ACK, so spicy!

—even the cooling sensation of mint.

Oooh, so cool!

Plus, they can warn us about potentially harmful foods.

Yuck! This apple is waaaaay too tart; it must not be ripe!

So we know you two are great at sensing danger, but let's talk about the *pleasure* of eating.

Yeah, this is hard work!

Let's have some FUN!

Think of your favorite food... if you're like me, you've got more than one.

*

pop

Us humans need to eat to survive, and many of the foods that we need also taste good.

But here's the catch—some of the foods that aren't so healthy taste good, too.

mmmpH

Sweet, greasy, fatty, and salty foods might taste great...

...but too much of them can be a bummer for your body.

Too many fatty foods can lead to unnecessary weight gain, as well as problems for your heart and liver.

And too much salt can cause high blood pressure and dehydration.

Too much sugar can increase your chance of cavities and cause weight gain as well.

*Cliché, but yes, the author's favorite food is pizza.

Okay, just one slice...

These types of foods should be eaten as a treat, and not every day.

Now, not everyone tastes food and drink the same way— your favorite food just may be someone else's LEAST favorite food.

Maybe you love green olives.

You ask your friend to try one. They take a bite, make a face, and spit it out!

!

How can you like THAT?! It tastes HORRIBLE!

KICK'D

TEXTURE (the way an object feels) can also be something that turns people off to food...

People say I'm too slimy...

...or too juicy...

...or too crunchy...

...or that I'm too leafy...

...or too mushy.

Despite liking— or not liking— certain foods, it's a good idea to try new foods.

As we age, our tastes can change.

A food that you used to hate might not taste so terrible anymore.

MUNCH MUNCH

Hey, these Brussels sprouts are all right!

Well, that about wraps it up for smell and taste.

Lend me your ears and I'll tell you all about...

HEARING!

eeee I'm awake!

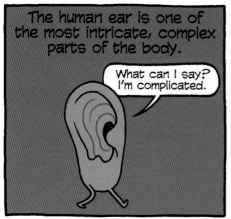

The human ear is one of the most intricate, complex parts of the body.

What can I say? I'm complicated.

For us to understand hearing, we must first understand SOUND.

Sound is created by VIBRATIONS...

...and these vibrations travel as SOUND WAVES.

Sound waves travel through air (or water) and once they reach our ears...

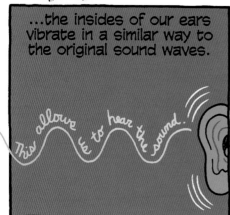

...the insides of our ears vibrate in a similar way to the original sound waves.

This allows E to hear the sound.

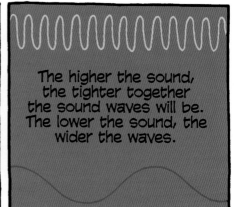

The higher the sound, the tighter together the sound waves will be. The lower the sound, the wider the waves.

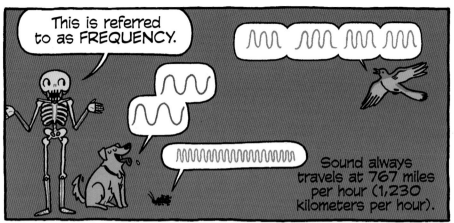

This is referred to as FREQUENCY.

Sound always travels at 767 miles per hour (1,230 kilometers per hour).

If you've ever heard your voice ECHO, you've heard sound traveling in action!

Your voice echoing back demonstrates how long it took...

...for sound waves to leave your mouth, bounce off an object, and travel back to you.

Some animals, like dogs, can hear higher-frequency sounds than humans.

Nice job!

Other animals, like bats and dolphins, even use sound to navigate!*

Now let's go INSIDE the ear to understand how it receives these sounds...

*This is called ECHOLOCATION

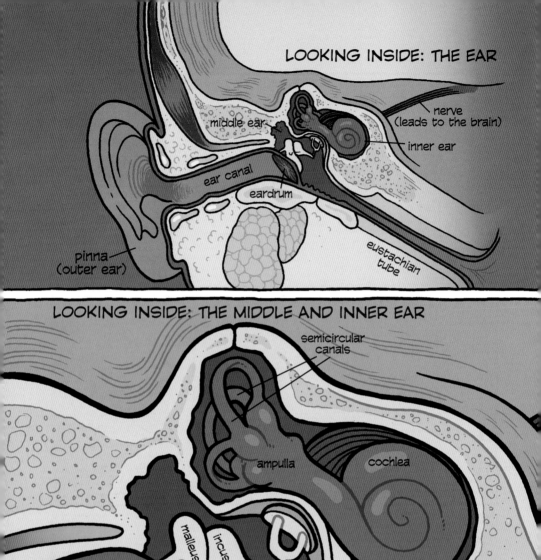

LOOKING INSIDE: THE EAR

nerve
(leads to the brain)

middle ear

inner ear

ear canal

eardrum

pinna
(outer ear)

eustachian
tube

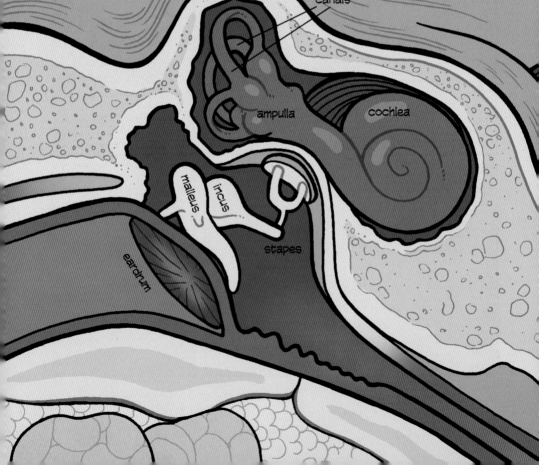

LOOKING INSIDE: THE MIDDLE AND INNER EAR

semicircular
canals

ampulla

cochlea

malleus

incus

stapes

eardrum

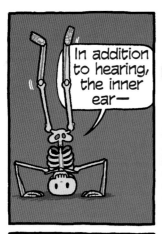 In addition to hearing, the inner ear—

 — helps us keep our balance and equilibrium.

 All that inner ear fluid gets sloshed around when we spin or do a handstand or cartwheel.

Inside the vestibule, there are sensory sacs called maculae.

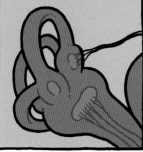

These jellylike sacs contain tiny hair cells attached to nerves, and they relay the position of the head to the brain.

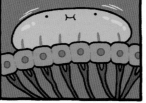

When you bend over, or do a cartwheel or a headstand, gravity pulls the jelly down, and the nerves pass that information to the brain.

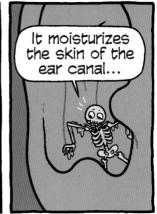

Our ears have ways of protecting themselves.

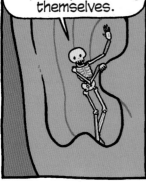

A waxy substance called EARWAX is secreted by glands in the outer ear canal.

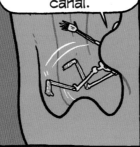

It moisturizes the skin of the ear canal...

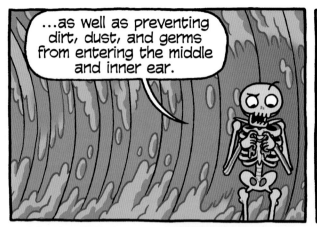

...as well as preventing dirt, dust, and germs from entering the middle and inner ear.

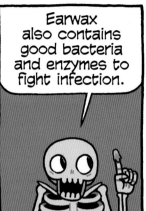

Earwax also contains good bacteria and enzymes to fight infection.

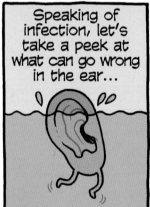

Speaking of infection, let's take a peek at what can go wrong in the ear...

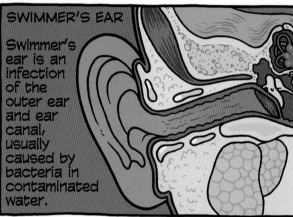

SWIMMER'S EAR

Swimmer's ear is an infection of the outer ear and ear canal, usually caused by bacteria in contaminated water.

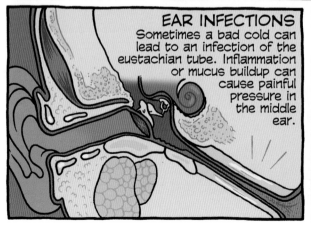

EAR INFECTIONS

Sometimes a bad cold can lead to an infection of the eustachian tube. Inflammation or mucus buildup can cause painful pressure in the middle ear.

Ear infections are more likely to affect children under the age of 5 because their eustachian tubes are shorter.

Bummer.

Here are some ways to keep your ears clean and healthy:

Each time you bathe or shower, wash your ears with warm soap and water.

Never stick anything bigger or smaller than your pinky finger in there—the internal parts of the ear are extremely sensitive.

Careful!

Use proper ear protection for loud noises.

Thanks!

Seems like you're pretty well taken care of!

All this safety can prevent damage like hearing loss.

Some people lack the ability to hear; this condition is known as DEAFNESS.

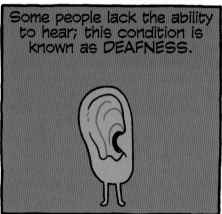

A person may become deaf due to hearing damage or an illness...

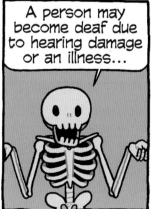

...or they may be born deaf.

Humans have developed a silent method of communication known as SIGN LANGUAGE.

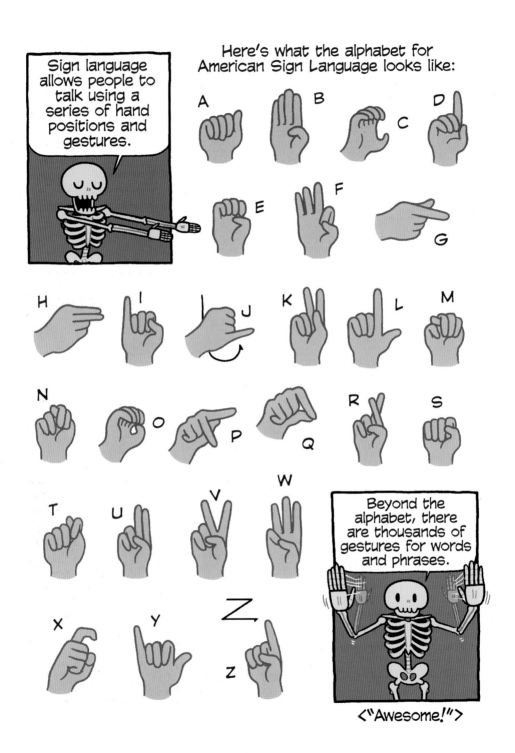

Sign language allows people to talk using a series of hand positions and gestures.

Here's what the alphabet for American Sign Language looks like:

<"Awesome!">

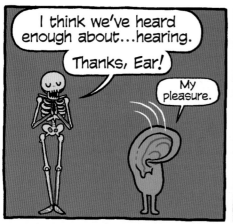

I think we've heard enough about...hearing.

Thanks, Ear!

My pleasure.

Let's look to our next sense...

SIGHT!

Sight is how we directly experience nearly everything in our environment.

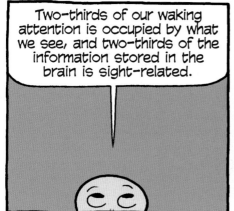

Two-thirds of our waking attention is occupied by what we see, and two-thirds of the information stored in the brain is sight-related.

In order to explain how the eyes see, we must first understand how LIGHT works.

Aah, my eye!

VISIBLE LIGHT is the light we see every day.

This light travels in a straight line unless it passes through glass, water, or, in this case, a prism.

Visible light is composed of the VISIBLE SPECTRUM.

RED
ORANGE
YELLOW
GREEN
BLUE
INDIGO
VIOLET

Here's how objects show color...

...like how this apple appears red:

That color—RED—is reflected back to your eye, while all the other colors are absorbed by the surface of the apple.

Mmm... red apple.

To understand how the eye actually sees color, let me first introduce you to the parts of the eye:

LOOKING INSIDE: THE EYE

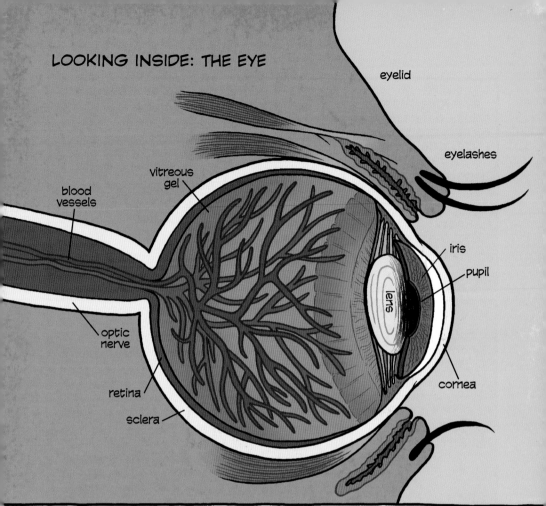

eyelid

eyelashes

vitreous gel

blood vessels

iris

pupil

lens

optic nerve

retina

sclera

cornea

The light reflected off the apple is received by the eye, but once inside—

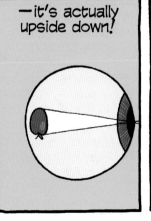

—it's actually upside down!

The optic nerve passes the image to the brain, where it is flipped right side up.

Just as everyone tastes things differently... people's eyes may see things differently.

COLOR BLINDNESS is an inability to detect color.

There are 2 types of color blindness: partial color blindness...

Hmm... That apple is...reddish brownish yellow?

...and total color blindness

I have absolutely NO idea what color this apple is...

Men are more likely to be color-blind than women, and you have a greater chance if one or both of your parents are color-blind.

But don't worry— if you are color-blind, it's not that big of a deal.

It just makes your art homework a little tricky...

...and you might have a harder time picking out matching clothes.

Sometimes parts of the eye are shaped in a way that makes it difficult to see clearly.

Uh, not quite like that.

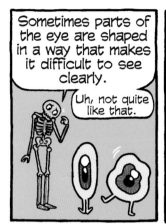

NEARSIGHTEDNESS—or MYOPIA—occurs when the light coming into the eye focuses in front of the retina, causing the image to be blurry.

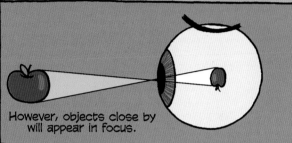

However, objects close by will appear in focus.

FARSIGHTEDNESS—or HYPEROPIA—occurs when the light coming into the eye focuses beyond the retina, making it difficult to see nearby objects.

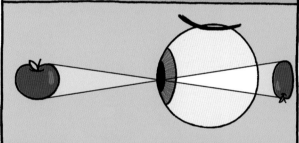

Both nearsightedness and farsightedness can be helped with the use of corrective lenses.

EYEGLASSES and CONTACT LENSES are both types of corrective lenses. Eyeglasses will look different depending on the condition:

Nearsightedness is corrected with a CONCAVE lense...

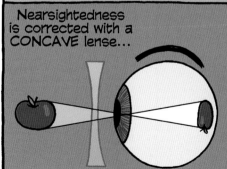

...while farsightedness is corrected with a CONVEX lens.

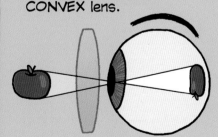

Glasses are great; they can even help to protect your eyes!

If you play a sport or are doing an activity that could possibly damage your eyes, I recommend safety goggles.

Us eyes come with built-in protection as well.

Tears aren't just for crying...

They keep the eyes moist, and contain enzymes that fight infection.

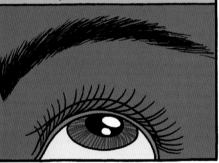

The surrounding eyelashes and eyebrows help keep the eyes safe, too!

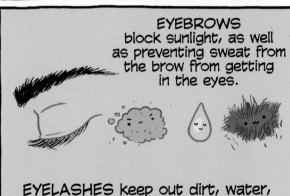

EYEBROWS block sunlight, as well as preventing sweat from the brow from getting in the eyes.

EYELASHES keep out dirt, water, sweat, hair...anything, really.

If you do get something in your eye, the best thing is to let your tears do their job or flush it out with warm water.

Despite all this protection, our eyes can still get infected—

AAAH-CHOO!

Um, you do know that eyes can't sneeze, right?

I don't feel so well...

CONJUNCTIVITIS is an eye infection that affects the outermost layer of the eye and the inner surface of the eyelids, making them pink in color.

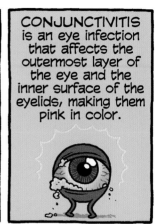

Conjunctivitis can be caused by a bacteria, a virus, or even an allergic reaction.

BWAHAHA! Remember us?

HA HA HA

Most cases of conjunctivitis will heal on their own...

ugh

feelin' better.

all better!

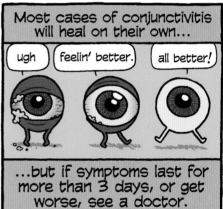

...but if symptoms last for more than 3 days, or get worse, see a doctor.

Conjunctivitis can be CONTAGIOUS and can spread easily from person to person.

AGH! Get away!

To prevent it, keep your face and eyes clean, and avoid touching your eyes with your hands.

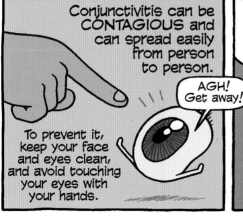

We've covered all sorts of eye stuff, but let's talk about what it's like to NOT have the sense of sight.

BLINDNESS is where a person lacks the ability to perceive light and/or objects.

This doesn't mean that all people who are blind see nothing; most can tell the difference between light and dark.*

Just like sign language for the deaf, people have developed a system to allow the blind to read...

...by using the sense of touch.

Braille is a touch-based alphabet system.

It uses a 2 x 3 grid.

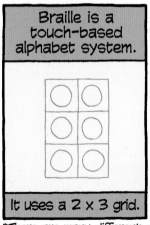

Each number and letter is formed by a specific pattern of raised dots.

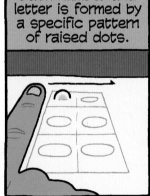

Numbers, letters, and words are read by running a finger across the Braille.

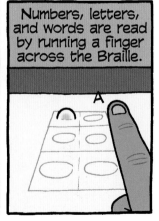

*There are many different degrees of blindness.

Here's a look at the Braille alphabet:

A ⠁   B ⠃   C ⠉   D ⠙   E ⠑   F ⠋

G ⠛   H ⠓   I ⠊   J ⠚   K ⠅   L ⠇

M ⠍   N ⠝   O ⠕   P ⠏   Q ⠟   R ⠗

S ⠎   T ⠞   U ⠥   V ⠧   W ⠺   X ⠭

Y ⠽   Z ⠵

Canes and guide dogs can also assist the blind and help them to find their way around.

When one sense is disabled or absent, the other senses step up and help out.

We're here to help!

Speaking of other senses, there's only one left...

TOUCH!
We can't talk about touch without talking about the body's largest organ:
SKIN!
Skin is a natural barrier that protects the inside of our bodies from dust, dirt, water, germs, and UV rays from the sun.
Get outta here!
Also, skin is like packaging for our muscles, guts, and bones.
Thanks!
But what's inside skin? Let's take a look:
HEY!

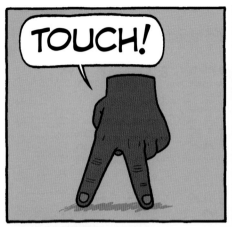

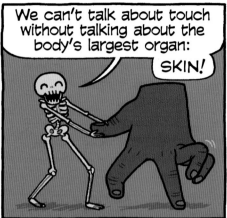

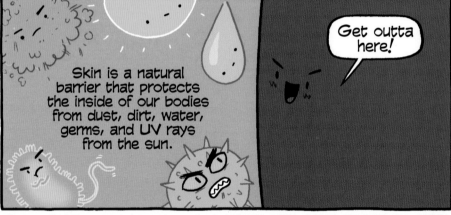

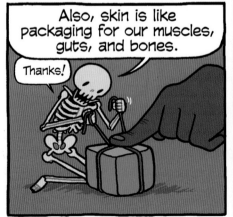

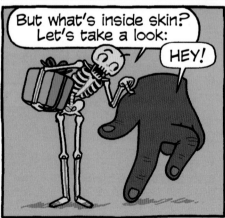

LOOKING INSIDE: SKIN

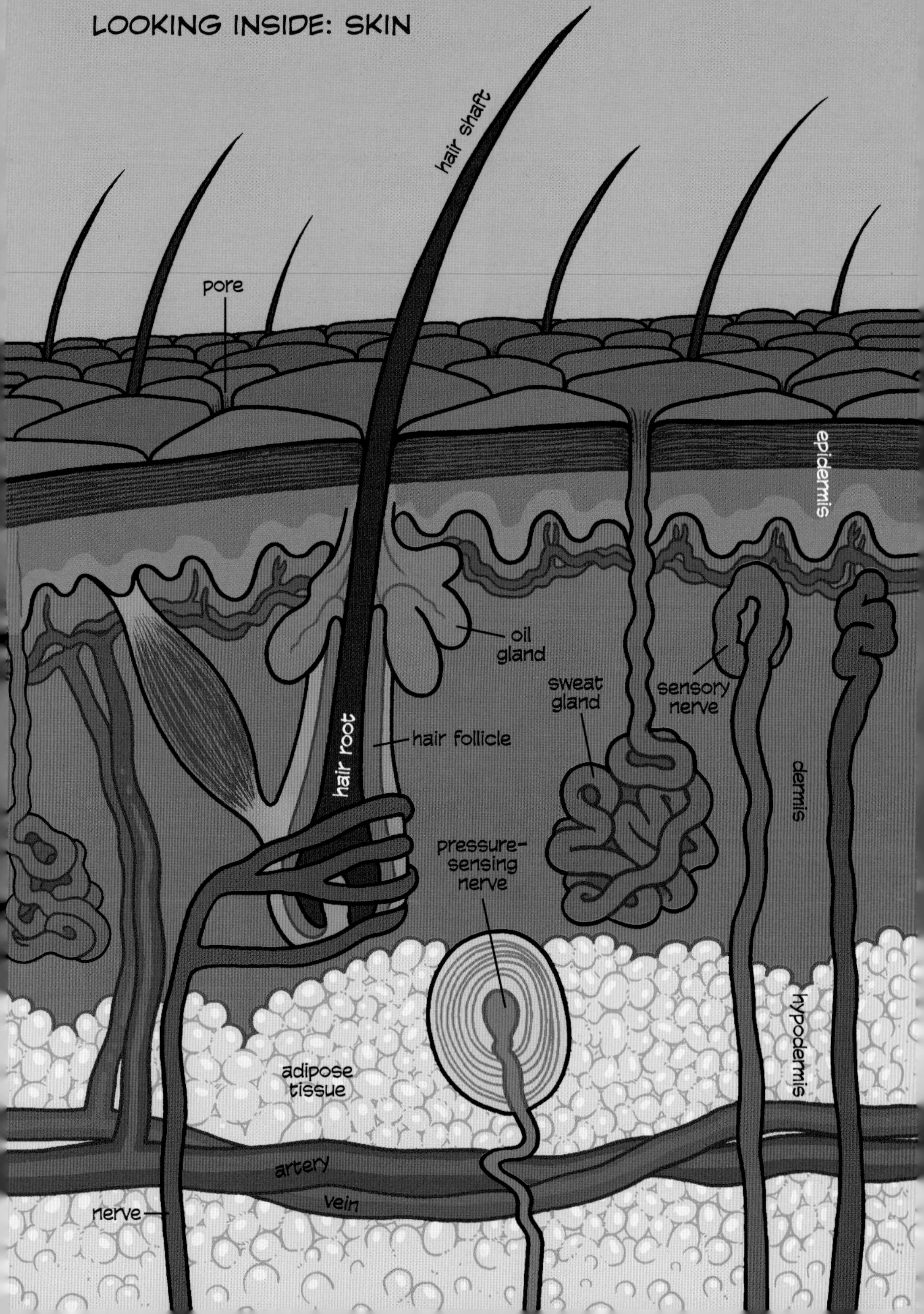
hair shaft
pore
epidermis
oil gland
sweat gland
sensory nerve
hair root
hair follicle
dermis
pressure-sensing nerve
hypodermis
adipose tissue
artery
vein
nerve

Hair follicles cover the whole body.

Humans have about 100,000 hairs on our heads...

...and about 3 million hairs covering the rest of the body.

Hair is made of a protein called KERATIN, and the hairs that we see are actually dead.*

Keratin is the same protein that is found in claws, hooves, horns, antlers, and our own fingernails and toenails.

SWEAT GLANDS release wastes, while OIL GLANDS secrete...oil.

The combination of these liquids and oils moistens the skin, helps us to grip objects, and keeps the skin from drying out.

Sweat contains water, urea, salts, sugars, and ammonia (which is leftover from the body breaking down protein).

This gives sweat its... unique smell.

Ugh, you stink!

Hmph. You've got some *nerve!*

*The base of the follicle, where the hair grows, is the only living part.

That's because I *am* a NERVE.

AAH! HOT!

Stop poking me!

OUCH!

Nerves in the skin serve as sensory cells. They alert the body (and brain) to changes in temperature, pressure, and pain.

This whole time, ADIPOSE (FATTY) TISSUE has stayed on the bottom, insulating the body.

Skin plays a key role in temperature regulation.

It can both RELEASE and RETAIN heat.

All courtesy of our sense of touch.

If we become too hot, our skin produces sweat. Sweat makes the skin wet and heat evaporates along with that sweat, cooling the body.

If we become cold, we might shiver or get "goose bumps" (or both).

Shivering gets the body to move, and movement generates warmth.

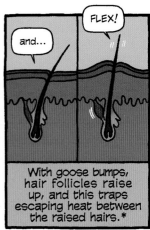

and...

FLEX!

With goose bumps, hair follicles raise up, and this traps escaping heat between the raised hairs.*

Our skin is most sensitive when we are young.

As us humans age, we lose sensitivity, especially in our hands.

Protect your skin by keeping it clean, eating healthy foods, and avoiding sunburns.

That doesn't mean avoiding the sun—

BOO!

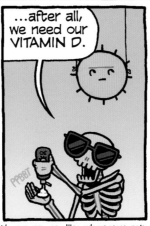

...after all, we need our VITAMIN D.

PPBBT

But if you are out in the sun for more than a half hour, be sure to protect your skin.

*Goose bumps also happen for other reasons, like when you get scared or feel emotion...and we don't know why this happens!

Overexposure to the sun's UV rays is harmful no matter what color your skin is.

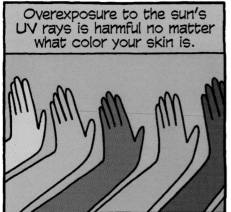

A SUNBURN damages our skin—and skin cells—right down to our DNA.

And repeated sunburns can mean permanent damage.

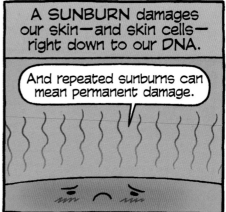

The sunburned top layer of skin cells die, and we wait for new ones to grow and replace them.

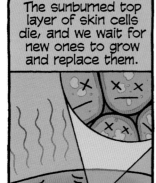

This is why sunburns take a week or two to heal (and it's also why they peel).

It's a good thing my cells are constantly renewing themselves!

A little sun exposure will actually help the skin protect itself from future sunburns.

Sun exposure produces a chemical called MELANIN in the skin.

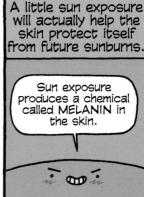

Melanin is a chemical called a PIGMENT, and it gives our skin its color.

It is also responsible for freckles...

...and moles.

(Not those kinds of moles.)

Protect your skin and help keep your largest organ happy and healthy.

Aw, thanks!

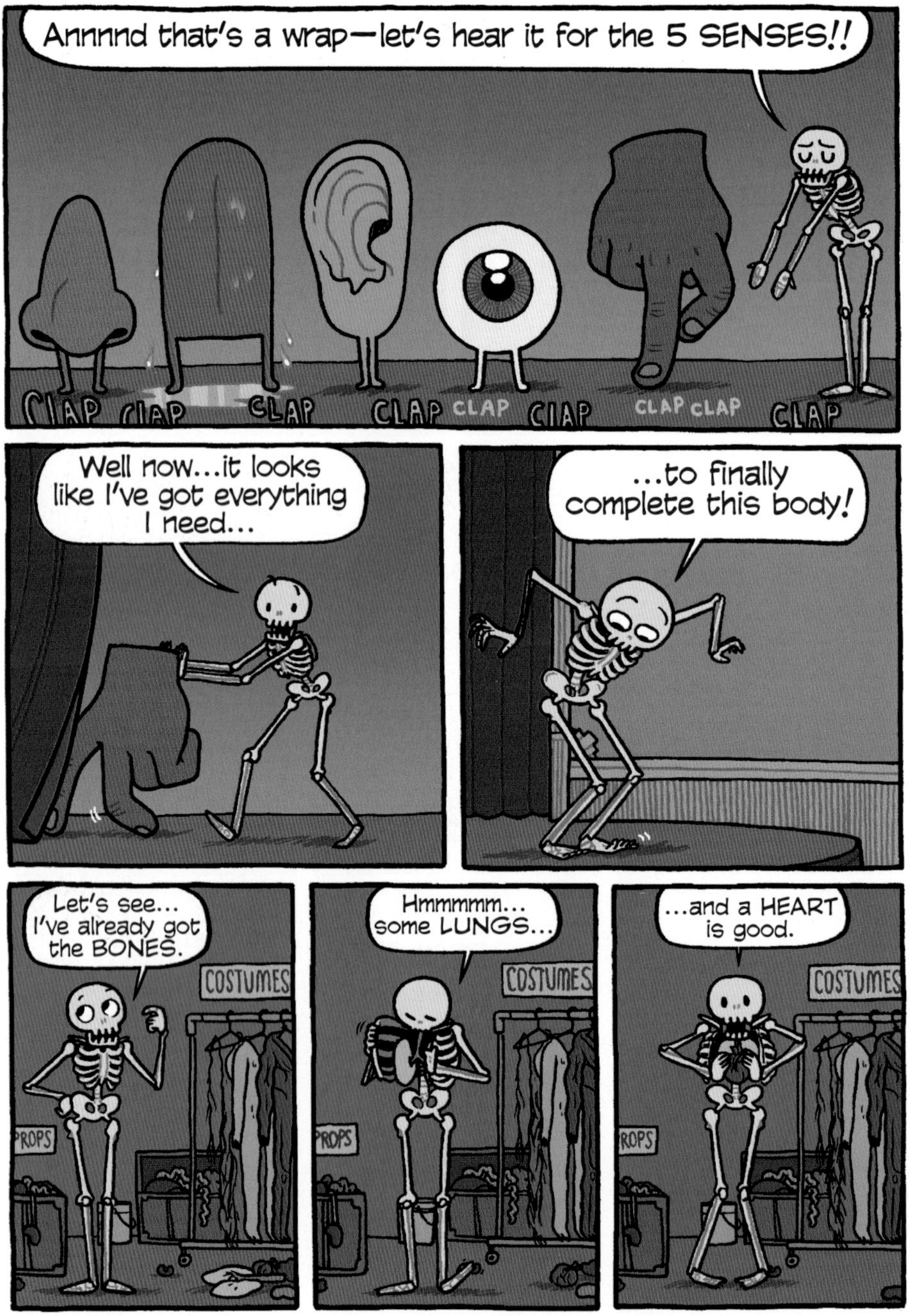
Annnnd that's a wrap—let's hear it for the 5 SENSES!!
CLAP CLAP CLAP CLAP CLAP CLAP CLAP CLAP CLAP
Well now...it looks like I've got everything I need...
...to finally complete this body!
Let's see... I've already got the BONES.
COSTUMES
PROPS
Hmmmmm... some LUNGS...
COSTUMES
PROPS
...and a HEART is good.
COSTUMES
PROPS

GUTS are great...
...as well as the KIDNEYS and BLADDER.
POKE POKE
We'll get all these GLANDS...
BUCKET 'O' GLANDS
...um, can I get a little privacy while I get my reproductive system in place?
COSTUMES
PROPS
Ick.
The IMMUNE SYSTEM.
So.
Much.
Mucus.
And, of course, the BRAIN.
Hello again, MUSCLES!
Huh.
I'm forgetting something...
Right!
SKIN!

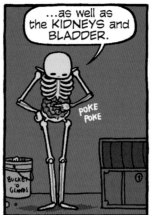

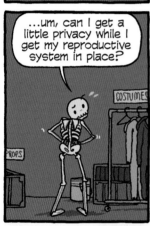

Uh—

—could I maybe get some clothes, please?

Aah, much better.

Ladies and gentlemen, I'd like to introduce you all to...well...

ME!

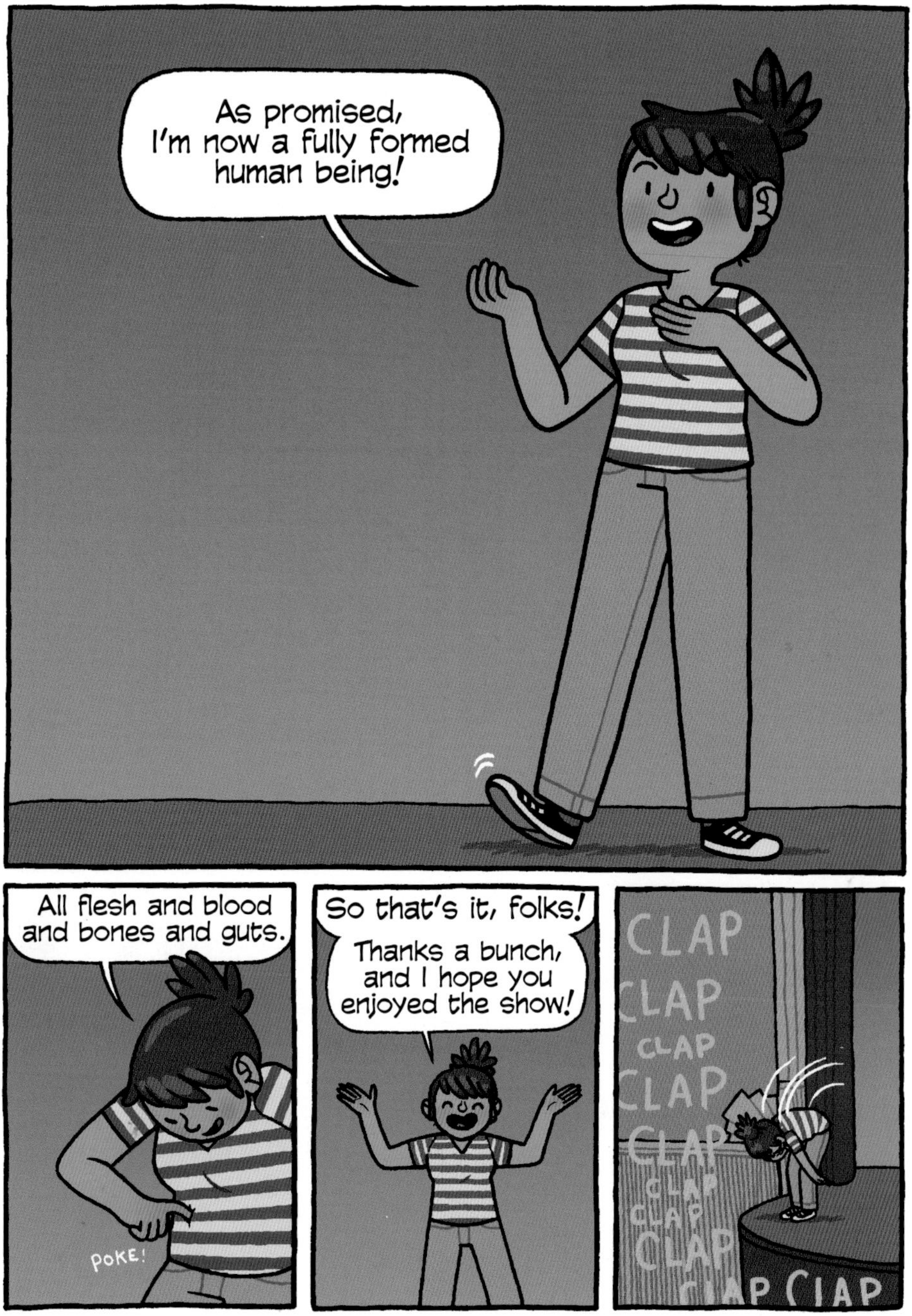
As promised, I'm now a fully formed human being!
All flesh and blood and bones and guts.
POKE!
So that's it, folks!
Thanks a bunch, and I hope you enjoyed the show!
CLAP
CLAP
CLAP
CLAP
CLAP

You're still here?

Okay, okay, there are a few more things, like an index, glossary... even a bibliography!

And if you want to keep learning about how totally awesome the human body is, I've included some other places to look.

All righty...

...bye-bye for real!

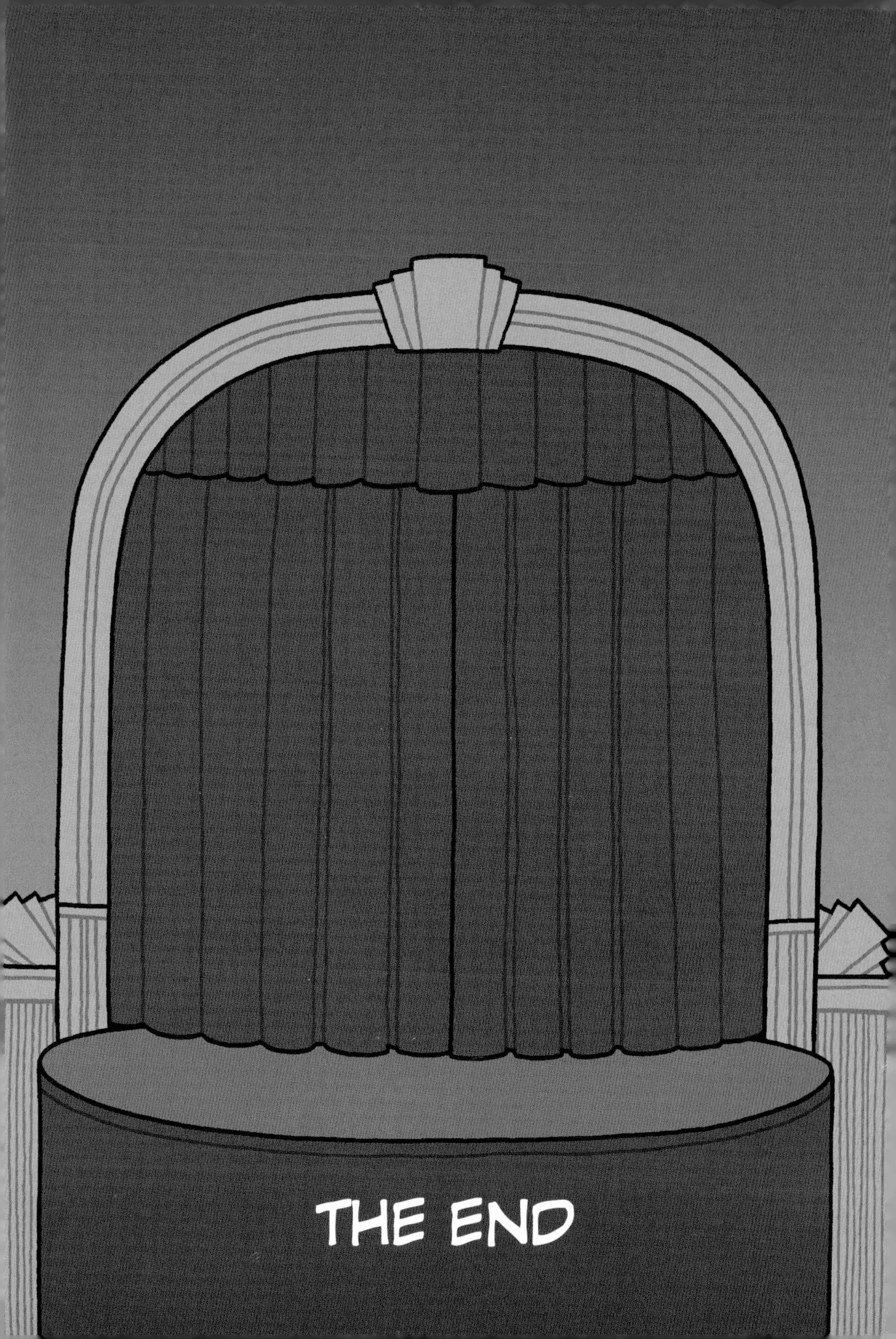
THE END

GLOSSARY

A

 **AIR** an invisible mixture of gases that surround our planet.

ALLERGY a condition that causes a person to become sick after eating, touching, or breathing something that is harmless to most people.

ALLERGEN the item that triggers an allergy.

ARTERY a blood vessel that carries blood away from the heart.

 ATOM the smallest unit of matter.

B

BACKBONE another name for spine.

BACTERIA a microscopic one-celled organism.

BLOOD the fluid that our heart pumps throughout our body.

BLOOD PRESSURE the measurement of force that our blood exerts against artery walls.

224

BOND a uniting or binding force.

BONES hard pieces that form the inside frame of an animal's body.

C

CAPILLARIES the smallest blood vessels in the human body.

CARBOHYDRATES a substance found in food that provides the body with energy.

CARDIAC MUSCLE muscle found in the heart.

CARTILAGE a strong, flexible material found throughout the body.

CELL a microscopic structure that combines with other cells to form a living thing.

CILIA tiny, hairlike structures.

CIRCULATE to move in a circle or course.

CLOT a clump made by blood as it thickens and sticks together.

COLLAGEN a strong, fibrous protein found throughout the body.

CONTRACT to tighten and make smaller.

E

ELEMENT — the name for each individual type of atom.

ENERGY — power made from nutrients.

ENZYME — a substance produced by a living thing that starts a chemical reaction.

EXHALATION/ EXPIRATION — to breathe out.

F

FATS — an oily or greasy substance that our bodies convert to energy.

FEVER — an abnormally high body temperature.

FIBER — a substance found in food that helps our body digest.

FRACTURE — a break (in a bone).

FUNGUS — an organism that survives on dead or decaying organisms.

G

GAS a substance that has no shape (like air).

GLAND a specialized group of cells in the body that sends and receives messages.

H

HEART the organ inside your chest that pumps blood throughout your body.

HEART RATE the number of times your heart beats per minute.

HORMONE a chemical produced by the body that gives instructions to another part of the body.

I

IMMUNIZATION the process by which a person's immune system is fortified against a bacteria or virus (through a shot/vaccine).

INFECTION a disease caused by germs that enter the body.

INFLAMMATION redness, heat, and swelling usually found around the site of an infection or reaction.

 INHALATION to breathe in.

INVERTEBRATE an animal without a spinal cord/backbone.

INVOLUNTARY an action done without conscious control.

J

JOINT the area where two bones meet.

L

LARGE INTESTINE the lower section of the digestive system, responsible for absorbing water and making poop.

LIGAMENT a band of tough, flexible tissue that attaches bone to bone, usually at the site of a joint.

LIQUID a substance that flows freely (like water).

LUNGS the organs that animals use to breathe air.

M

MOLECULE one or more atoms hanging out together.

MUCUS a slimy substance made by various areas of the body (think: snot).

MUSCLE a body tissue that can expand and contract; responsible for our movement.

N

NERVE a band of tissue that helps the nervous system relay messages throughout the body.

NEURON a nerve cell.

NUTRIENT a substance that provides nourishment and energy to the body.

O

ORGANISM a living thing.

ribbit!

PROTEINS

P

PROTEINS a substance found in foods that our body converts to energy.

PROTOZOA a microscopic animal, many of which are capable of making humans sick.

PUBERTY the physical and emotional transition from childhood to adulthood.

PULSE regular throbbing in the arteries, caused by the beating of the heart.

R

RELAX to make or become loose.

S

SCAB a crust of hardened blood that forms over and protects a wound.

SCAR the mark left on the skin after a wound has healed.

SKELETON	the supporting framework for a living thing.
SKELETAL MUSCLES	the muscles that help us move our body.
SMALL INTESTINE	the middle section of the digestive system, responsible for absorbing nutrients from food.
SOLID	a substance that is hard.
SPINAL CORD	cord of nerve tissue that extends from the brain and runs along the backbone/spine.
SPINE	the series of bones that extend down the back; responsible for protecting the spinal cord.
SPRAIN	a twisting or tearing of a ligament.
STRAIN	a twisting or overstretching of a muscle.
STOMACH	the organ that digests food.
SUGARS	a substance found in foods that our body converts to energy.

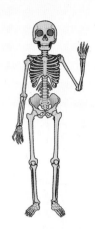

T

TEMPERATURE   the degree of hotness or coldness of something.

TENDON   a band of tough, flexible tissue that connects muscle to bone.

TISSUE   a collection of cells that forms a larger structure in the body.

V

VALVE   a flap found in blood vessels that closes temporarily to prevent backflow of blood.

VERTEBRA   one of the single bones that make up the spine.

VERTEBRATE   an animal that has a spinal cord/backbone.

VIRUS   a microscopic infectious organism.

VISCERAL MUSCLE   the muscle that makes up the body's vital organs.

VOLUNTARY   an action done with conscious control.

BIBLIOGRAPHY and RECOMMENDED READING

Macaulay, David. *The Way We Work: Getting to Know the Human Body*. Boston: Houghton Mifflin Company, 2008.

Clayman, Charles, MD. *The Human Body: An Illustrated Guide to its Structure, Function, and Disorders*. New York: Dorling Kindersley Publishing, 1995.

Parker, Steve. *Human Body*. New York: Dorling Kindersley Publishing, 1993.

kidshealth.org/kid/

kids.usa.gov/health-and-safety/health

Thanks to the fantastically wrinkly brains
of Cyrus Yau and Sara Lasser Yau,
Will Lupens, Paolo Rivera, Dave Jordan
& Loryn Udell, and Joe Quinones for
reading and giving me feedback on
Human Body Theater in all of its
various stages of development.

Thanks to my family, and especially
my sister Leslie and all of her
first aid follies.

Thanks to all the wonderful folks at
First Second; without them, this book
would not be possible.

—Maris